PAPERCRAFT

PAPERCRAFT

MOIRA BUTTERFIELD

CHARTWELL
BOOKS, INC.

A QUARTO BOOK

Published by Chartwell Books
A Division of Book Sales, Inc.
PO Box 7100
Edison, New Jersey 08818-7100

This edition produced for sale in the U.S.A., its
territories and dependencies only.

ISBN 0-7858-0635-0

This book was designed and produced by
Quarto Children's Books Ltd
The Fitzpatrick Building
188-194 York Way
London N7 9QP

Project Editor Simon Beecroft
Designer Matthew Gore
Editor Jane Havell
Photographers Laura Wickenden and Colin Bowling
Indexer Hilary Bird

Creative Director Louise Jervis
Senior Art Editor Nigel Bradley

The publishers would like to thank Jayne Evans, Jonathan Gilbert, Lisa Hollis,
Bernard Nussbaum, and Geoff Rayner for their artistic input.

Manufactured by Bright Arts (Singapore) PTE Ltd, Singapore
Printed by Star Standard Industries (PTE) Ltd, Singapore

Contents

All about paper 10

Start here 12

Folds and fans 14

Fans and concertinas 16

Quilling 18

Perfect planes 20

Beautiful boats 22

Paper people 24

Letter lady 26

Pop-up cards 28

Cards for fun 30

Poster cards 32

Paper collages 34

Collage frames and mosaics 36

Paper weaving 38

Woven baskets 40

Perfect pricking 42

Toys and games 44

Party table 46

Party decorations 48

Boxes and bags 50

Storage boxes 52

Papier mache molds 54

Papier mache models 56

Stationery shop 58

Personal stationery 60

Tissue flowers 62

Puppets and kites 64

Handy hats 66

Fancy dress hats 68

Fancy dress clothes 70

Shirts and waistcoats 72

Mask magic 74

More amazing masks 76

Decorating paper 78

Special stitching 80

Origami 82

Origami butterfly 84

Craft festivities 86

Papermaking 88

Finishing paper 90

Index 92

All about paper

Paper is made from wood, plant, or rag fibers, and was invented in China over 2,000 years ago. The ideas in this book will introduce you to a world of new paper art possibilities. It's a good idea to learn about basic techniques, but remember you can also have a lot of fun experimenting.

Finding the grain

When paper is made mechanically, its fibers tend to line up in one direction. This is called the "grain." Paper folds, tears, and bends more easily in this direction. For complicated projects involving paper-folding, it is often important to find the grain before you start.

Different paper and card

Generally, the stronger paper is, the better it will be at holding a crease or fold, which is important for paper art. There's a wide range of paper and card you can use. Here we show you some of the main types – all of them are easy to buy.

▶ *Crepe paper is stretchy and crinkly. You can buy it in lots of colors.*

◀ *Japanese paper is thin but very strong, because it is made from long fibers.*

◀ *Medium-weight paper, such as ordinary writing paper, can be painted if it has an absorbent, dull ("matt") surface.*

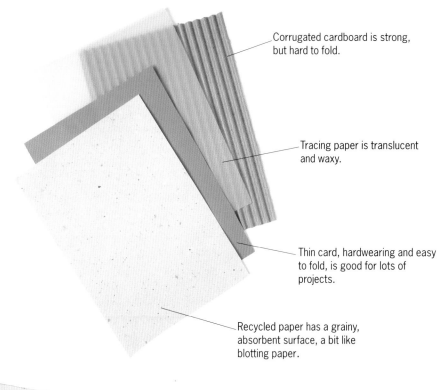

Corrugated cardboard is strong, but hard to fold.

Tracing paper is translucent and waxy.

Thin card, hardwearing and easy to fold, is good for lots of projects.

Recycled paper has a grainy, absorbent surface, a bit like blotting paper.

◀ *Tissue paper is thin, see-through, and delicate. It tears easily.*

◀ *Handmade paper is thick, with many different kinds of decorative surface.*

◀ *Stencil card is a kind of waxy, thin cardboard, that won't absorb water.*

PAPERCRAFT TOOLS

Here are the main tools needed for the projects in this book. A sturdy metal ruler is better than a plastic one, and safer when you are using a knife. A cutting mat, to protect the surface of your desk or table, can be made of plastic, or you can make your own from several layers of cardboard glued or taped together. Always work on a cutting mat when using a craft knife.

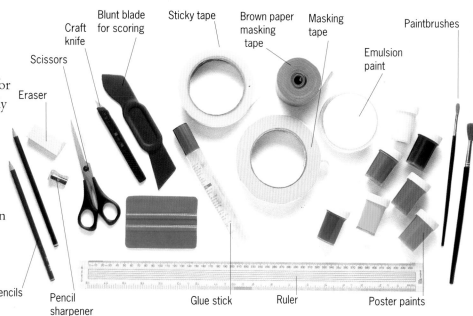

Blunt blade for scoring

Craft knife

Sticky tape

Brown paper masking tape

Masking tape

Paintbrushes

Scissors

Emulsion paint

Eraser

Pencils

Pencil sharpener

Glue stick

Ruler

Poster paints

Start here

MOST OF THE IDEAS FEATURED in this book use one or more of these basic techniques. Spend a few minutes practicing each one before you go on to more ambitious projects. Whatever you try, always remember the most important rule of papercraft: "Don't rush it!"

FOLDING

It's a good idea to make folds by laying your paper against a hard surface, such as the top of a table. This helps you to get a neat edge.

▶ *A fold that peaks upwards into an upside-down V-shape is called a "mountain fold."*

▶ *A fold that dips down into a V-shape is called a "valley fold."*

SCORING

Scoring weakens thick paper or card slightly along a line on one side, so it is easier to make a straight, sharp fold. Always score on the side of the paper that will be on the inside.

PLEATING

Lots of parallel score lines close together enable you to make paper pleats. Practice on square piece of paper, and then on a round piece.

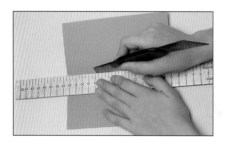

1 *With a ruler as a guide, run the end of a pair of scissors along your fold line.*

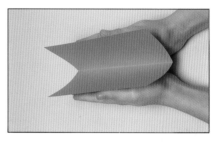

2 *Bend along the scored line. The paper or card will hold the fold neatly in place.*

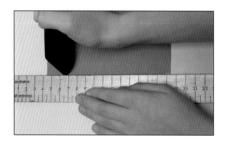

1 *Mark the top and bottom of each fold line, to guide the ruler as you score.*

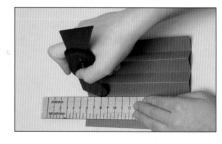

2 *Turn the paper over after each score line, so that you make pleats.*

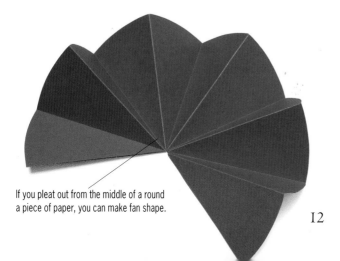

If you pleat out from the middle of a round a piece of paper, you can make fan shape.

Scoring alternately on each side of the paper means you make mountain folds followed by valley folds (see above).

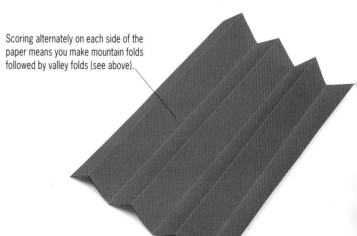

CURLING

You can use curled paper for all kinds of projects, including paper hair, present decorations, and 3D pictures. Thin paper is easier to curl than thick paper.

I Wind a long paper strip tightly round a pencil. Keep it wound up tightly for a minute or so, holding it in place with your finger and thumb.

Use paper curls for hair and eyebrows.

2 Release the paper. If the curl is not tight enough, lay the pencil across the front of the paper, and pull the strip gently toward you under the pencil a few times.

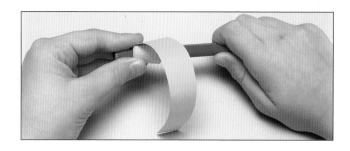

▲ *Depending on how hard you wind the paper, you can make loose curls...*

▲ *...or tight curls. This gives a variety of different effects in your pictures.*

CUTTING

To cut holes out of paper you need small sharp scissors, or a craft knife for more complicated shapes. If you use a craft knife you must use a hard board or a cutting mat (see page 11), to prevent damaging the surface underneath. To cut accurately, pencil guidelines lightly on the paper before you start.

◀ *This night scene is backed with shiny silver paper (you could use foil) to give a glittering effect.*

Cut a small cross shape into the paper and open out the flaps for stars.

If you are using scissors, keep cut-out shapes simple.

Folds and fans

WHEN PAPER IS PLEATED, EACH MOUNTAIN FOLD IS followed by a valley fold. In other words, you must fold first to one side of the paper and then the other. You will get the most accurate effect if you measure the folds to keep them even, and score the fold lines (see page 12), but it's not absolutely necessary. Start by practicing pleats on scrap paper, and then try some of the projects shown here.

PLEAT CUTTING

If you cut into pleated paper, you can make very interesting shapes and patterns. Experiment with different shapes, and then push in or pull out the paper in between the cuts. Think of ways you might use these effects on a greetings card, poster, or painting, perhaps by mounting the pleats on contrasting paper.

WHAT YOU NEED

A3 sheet of stiff, colored paper

Small, sharp scissors

A3 sheet of mounting paper
in a contrasting color

Glue

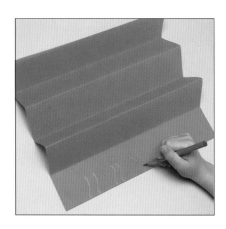

1 *Make marks evenly and lightly across the width of a pleated sheet of paper. These will be a guide for where to make decorative cuts through the pleats.*

2 *Pinch together a pleat and cut into it. Start with some straight cuts, then make cuts of different shapes on each pleat. Try zigzags, curves, and sloping cuts.*

3 *Open the cuts gently, taking care not to tear the paper. Mount your pleated "picture" on a contrasting color of card, so that the pattern shows through.*

FOLDED FLOWERS

Pleated paper makes good, simple flower shapes. To display them in a vase, glue the flower "heads" onto circles of card. Then glue two circles together back to back, with a plant stick in between so that they stand up.

WHAT YOU NEED

Medium weight colored paper – good-quality wrapping paper sugar paper, or any paper that will hold a pleat

Glue and brush

Tissue paper for the flower centers

Sharp scissors

Paint, brushes, and mounting paper

Card circles and plant sticks for vase display

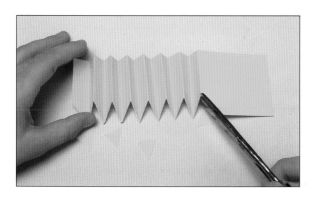

1 Cut two strips of paper each about 2 x 16 inches. Make 0.5-inch pleats along the narrow edges of both strips of paper. With sharp scissors, snip a corner off the top of each pleat. Open up the pleated strips. Curve them round so that they make circles, and glue them together at both ends.

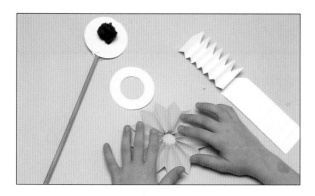

2 When they are dry, mount them on circles of card. Glue two flower circles together, back to back, with a thin plant stick in between. Last, screw up little balls of contrasting tissue paper and glue these to the centers of the flowers.

Pleated paper looks like flower heads

Use thin. light plant sticks for the stalks

Tissue paper balls make the centers

▶ *Stand your flowers in a vase to display them to best effect.*

15

Fans and concertinas

Pleated paper can be used for all kinds of things, from a simple decorative fan to a card! These cards are called "concertinas" because the folds look like the middle part of the musical instrument.

WHAT YOU NEED

Piece of thin card 25 x 7 inches
Scissors, ruler, and pencil
Hard surface on which to work
Crayons, felt-tips, or paints

CONCERTINA CARD

The card here is made with a jungle theme, but you can change that to any subject you like by cutting the pages into different shapes and painting different pictures. Concertina cards make very good celebration cards, and they stand up on their own.

1 *Measure along the card's long edges, making marks every 5 inches on the top and bottom. Score between the first pair of marks. Turn the card over, and score between the next pair of marks.*

2 *Turn over again for the third pair, and over again for the last. Then fold the card up in this order – valley fold, mountain fold, valley fold, mountain fold. This will give a zig-zag effect.*

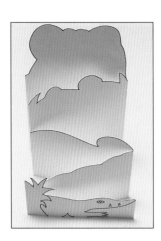

3 *On the smallest fold, draw a seated animal no taller than 2 inches. Cut round the shape to the folded spine and fold the card up again. Repeat on the next fold but this time make your animal a bit bigger than the last one – they should each look over the last one's shoulder!*

4 *Using your crayons, felt tips, or paints, decorate the paper concertina. Here we have used greens for a jungle scene, and painted it full of colorful animals.*

Add jungle animals to your forest scene

The crocodile makes a good front cover!

Fabulous fans

Pleated paper fans have been made for centuries. Here are some ways you can make your own elegant versions. You can use any paper as long as it holds a pleat well. If you like, paint colorful pictures on your paper before you start.

WHAT YOU NEED

A3 sheet of paper

Glue

Pretty thread, ribbon, or piping braid

Hole puncher

Sharp scissors

1 Pleat a rectangle of colorful paper along the long edge, starting and finishing with a mountain fold. The pleats shown here are 0.75 inches wide.

2 Bunch the pleats together, and fold the strip over at the center. Bring the two long edges together so that they touch, then glue them together from top to bottom.

3 To make decorative holes, pinch the fan pleats together and snip small triangles evenly out of the front edges. Tie the bottom with ribbon or braid.

4 Open out the fan. Trim back the glued seam so that it does not show through the center hole when the fan is open.

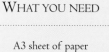

A neat hole punched through the end makes it easier to tie tightly with some ribbon.

If you like, thread some pretty braid or ribbon through the holes for a final decoration.

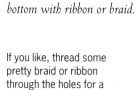

A fan decorated with beautiful ribbon makes a special present.

Quilling

Quilling means winding strips of colored paper into different-shaped coils. You can use them for decoration, and even for making pictures. It takes a little while to do, but it's great fun and very satisfying!

Make your paper quills into whatever shapes you like.

QUILLING PICTURES

Quilling pictures are best made with subjects that have curvy shapes that can be easily quilled — circles and ovals, for example. But you can always draw and paint some details and use quilling for others. First, sketch out your picture roughly on medium-weight card and make all the tight and loose coils you need. Glue them to the picture and then finish it off.

▲ Trees make good subjects for quilling patterns. Birds, sheep with curly fleece, peacock tails, and fish are also ideal.

1 Make two slits about 0.25 inch deep in the top of a straw.

2 Slot one end of your paper strip into the slits and wind the strip round and round the straw.

▲ Make pretty gift tags by sticking coils onto folded card.

PHOTO FRAME

You can adapt quilling to decorate a cardboard frame for your favorite photograph.

WHAT YOU NEED

Two pieces of medium-weight colored card, each 6 x 8 inches

Glue and glue brush

Ruler and pencil

Colored paper quilling strips

Sharp scissors, or craft knife and cutting board

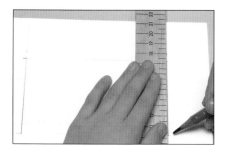

1 On one piece of card measure an area that is the same size as the photograph you want to display in the frame. Make sure to leave an outer margin around it of about 1.5 inches.

2 On the second piece of contrasting card, mark out the same area and cut the central part out carefully using a craft knife with a cutting mat underneath to protect your work surface.

3 Arrange the quilling on the frame. Brush glue to the back of the coils and fix them in place. Use tweezers to place them exactly where you want them, then press down gently but firmly.

▲ *Run a thin line of glue along three edges of the back of the frame and press it carefully down onto the piece of backing card. When it is dry, slide in your photo through the unglued edge.*

Perfect planes

Use your paper-folding skills to become an airplane inventor. Try the basic designs shown here and then build on them by adding tails, cutting flaps, or folding the paper slightly differently to get varying nose and wing shapes. Flight-test your inventions to see how they perform!

WHAT YOU NEED

Rectangle of paper, light but strong

DART AND STUNT PLANE

As a paper plane travels, air pushes up against the wings. The basic dart is a sharp, streamlined shape, so it slices through the air fast and straight like an arrow. The stunt plane, with wider wings, floats rather than flies, and travels for a longer distance. To get pinpoint accuracy, score the creases first.

DART

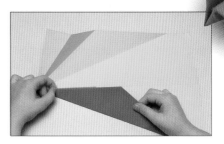

1 *Fold the paper in half lengthwise. Unfold it and fold one corner into the middle so that the edge meets the crease.*

2 *Fold the other corner in to meet the center crease, making sure you keep the point at the top neat and sharp.*

3 *Keeping the folds you have made in place, fold the same corners down to the middle again.*

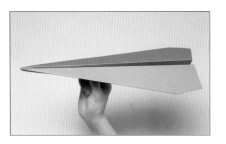

4 *Turn the paper over, and fold it up along the original center crease mark. To fly the dart, hold it underneath and launch it upwards.*

Experiment with different-shaped rectangles of paper to get different flight paths!

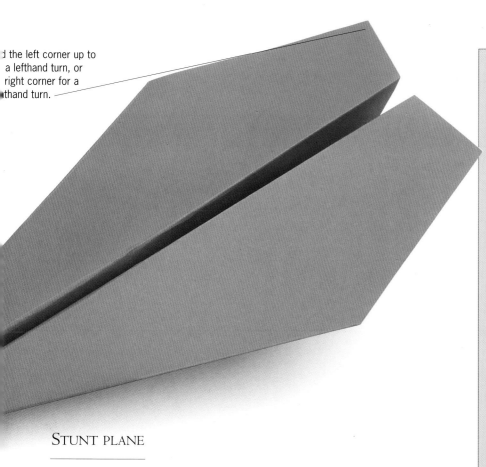

the left corner up to a lefthand turn, or right corner for a thand turn.

STUNT PLANE

By adding a tail or flaps, you can alter the way the air acts on your plane to make it do different stunts.

1 *Follow steps 1 and 2 of the dart, then fold the triangle over. Fold the two new top corners into the center to make a flat end at the top.*

2 *Fold the center point up to make a tab. You can unfold the top corners when doing this, as here, but you must fold them over again and under the tab.*

3 *Fold the two outer edges into the central crease, leaving the flat top. Take time to do this accurately so that all the folds are sharp and straight.*

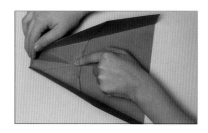

4 *Fold outward along the center crease. When you turn the stunt plane over, unfold the wings. It will look like the finished dart at the top of the page.*

SPINNING HELICOPTER

Drop this helicopter down from a height and watch it spin fast as it falls. It's one of the quickest and easiest toys you can make!

WHAT YOU NEED

Strip of thin card 1 x 3.5 inches long
Scissors or craft knife
Ruler
Paper clip

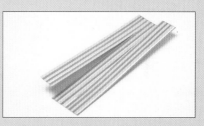

1 *Cut two straight 3-inch slits in the card, one on either side.*

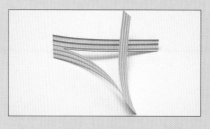

2 *Hold the top right corner and the bottom left corner. Pull them together to make a triangle shape.*

3 *Push the paper clip up over the two ends. Drop the helicopter with the paper clip pointing downwards.*

Beautiful boats

WITH A FLOTILLA OF BRIGHTLY decorated paper boats you and your friends can hold your own racing regatta! Line the boats up on a smooth floor, and flap a magazine up and down behind them to create enough breeze to get them going.

WHAT YOU NEED

Rectangle of thin but strong paper that holds creases well
Sticky tape

PAPER BOAT

Experiment with different-sized rectangles to get different-shaped boats, all using the same basic design. Practice using newspaper before you move onto more high-quality paper.

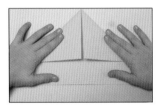

1 *Fold the rectangle in half widthwise. With the fold at the top, turn the two top corners down to the center.*

2 *Fold up one bottom edge to make a flap. Turn the boat over and fold up the other edge to make another flap.*

3 *Fold the corners back on either side and tape them flat. You need to turn the boat over to do the underside flap.*

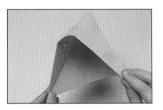

4 *Hold the taped corners and push them together (halfway through this stage you have a Robin Hood hat!).*

5 *You should then have a square with two triangular flaps. Fold up the flaps on either side to the top.*

6 *Now you should have a triangle. Push the lower corners together to make the flat square shown above.*

▶ *To finish off your boat, press the base flat and pull out the sides to give it the shape shown here.*

7 *Pull the top points apart sideways. You should then see a triangular "sail" pop out from the base of the boat.*

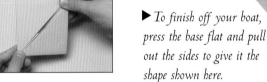

Sail stands up straight from the base of the boat

RIGGED SAILING SHIP

This ship has sails made from fine, cream-colored paper to look like real canvas. First draw or paint a ship on the background paper, including the masts and the rigging (all the ropes), but leaving off the sails that are fixed to the masts.

WHAT YOU NEED

Good-quality thick paper for sails
Thick, rubbery-textured glue and glue brush
Pencil, scissors, and ruler
Fine felt-tips or paints
Rectangle of good-quality paper for background
Piece of card to mount the picture

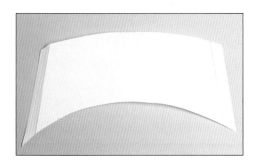

I *First sketch your sail shape, then cut it out with some extra at each side. Fold back the extra width to make tabs. Make big, medium and small sails, and decorate them if you like.*

2 *Fold back the tabs on either side of the sails. Brush these with glue and stick the sails on your picture so they curve outwards. For a finishing touch, mount your picture on contrasting card, smoothing it flat.*

Paper people

IT'S EASY TO MAKE PAPER PEOPLE, USING PAPER SCRAPS or card cut from empty food packets. Use them as decorations (in a Christmas crib scene, for example) or as 3D works of art. To give them character, add paper clothes and facial features such as paper noses. When you have practiced a bit with basic shapes, use your imagination to create your own unique people.

WHAT YOU NEED

Paper thin enough to bend

Ruler

Selection of paper scraps

Glue and glue brush

Sticky tape

Scissors

Compass and pencil

CONE PERSON

Make cone-shaped bodies from paper and stick on contrasting-colored paper pieces for decoration, clothes, and hair. You can also paint on clothes and funny faces.

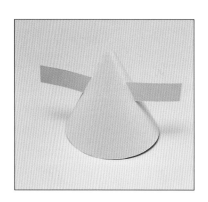

1 Cut a semi-circle of paper and curve it round in a cone. Mark arm positions, open out the paper and cut two small arm slits. Curve the cone again and tape the edges together, then slot through a strip for the arms.

2 Make a smaller cone for the head and glue on curled strips of paper for hair (see page 13). Make a skirt by pleating a curved strip of colored paper and glueing it round the cone body. Paint or draw on a face.

CYLINDER PERSON

The cylinder person is made in a similar way to the cone person, but with a straight strip of paper that makes a tube shape when curved round. Always check details like armhole positions before you tape the person together at the back.

1 Cut a paper strip and curve it round into a tube, with an arm strip slotted in as for the cone person above. Make a slightly smaller cylinder for the head and glue it in place.

2 Curve two strips of paper into tubes for the legs, and glue them to the inside of the body. For a hat, make the head extra long, then push a circle of paper down on it for the brim.

Why not display your figures in a toy theater? Cut out one of the big sides of a cereal packet – the remaining three sides make a good stage! Glue paper pieces onto the back and sides to make scenery. Then place your figures in position on the base.

▼ *This chapel scene has a "stained glass" window in the background made from pieces of colored tissue paper. It looks very effective when light shines through!*

Hair is made from curled strips of paper.

Draw your own funny faces!

Buttons are made from circles of paper, slit to the center, and curved round in shallow cone shapes.

Letter Lady

Paper people can be useful as well as decorative. Here we show you how to make a letter lady to store your mail, and some unusual pieces of paper jewelry to wear, and give your friends as presents.

LETTER LADY

This letter holder lady is made from stiff card decorated with paint and brightly colored paper. To make her look realistic, add a paper cone nose and a collar frill. Instead of a stand, you could make a hole in her hat and hang her on the wall or your pinboard. Store letters or pens and pencils in her pocket.

1 *Cut out one big side of a cereal box, together with one of the attached narrow edges to make a stand. Draw a figure on the blank side and cut round it. Decorate the lady with cut-out paper pieces, or paint her. Fold the flap to the back along the crease so that it makes a base enabling her to stand upright.*

2 *Cut out one side of a shallow box, leaving a narrow margin before all the folded edges. Cut off one narrow edge completely. The margin round three sides make tabs that you can glue to the lady's skirt. The narrow edges give you a pocket big enough to put things in.*

3 *For a stand, bend the flap at the bottom of the lady's skirt to the back, so that she stays upright.*

MINI-PEOPLE

These mini-people, made from card and fabric, are based on traditional jewelry made in South America. Here, they have been used as decoration on a triangular-shaped badge and a matching necklace.

WHAT YOU NEED

Strips of paper 6 x I inches

Scraps of fabric (cut with pinking shears to stop the edges fraying)

PVA glue

Felt-tip pens

Card (cut from an old packing box)

Safety pin or badge bar

Sticky tape

I *Wrap a strip of thin card into a tight cylinder and tape it in place. Glue a strip of fabric or ribbon round the card cylinder, leaving a short length of card sticking up. Draw a face on this. Make enough mini-people to cover the size you want your badge and necklace to be.*

2 *Cut the card into badge and necklace shapes. Paint them and cover them with PVA glue. Stick your mini-people onto them. When the badge is dry, tape or glue a safety pin or badge bar on the back. Punch a hole in each end of the necklace and thread it with cotton to tie round your neck.*

This slot is for storing letters in.

This is a good way to use up scraps of brightly colored ribbon.

Pop-up cards

MAKE YOUR OWN CARDS TO GIVE at celebration times. Use your imagination to make designs that are particularly suited to the people who will receive them. They will be extra-special because you've taken time and trouble over them! You can use the ideas in this section to make unusual art pictures, too.

POP-UPS

There are two basic techniques for making pop-up pictures. Practice them both on scrap paper before you design your own card. Wherever the instructions tell you to fold a line, remember to score it first (see the instructions on page 12).

CUTTING METHOD

1 Fold over a rectangle of card. Use a pencil and ruler to mark two equal lines at right angles to the central crease. Cut into these lines through both layers of card.

2 Fold the section between the cuts over to the left and crease it. Then unfold it again and open up the card.

3 Inside the card, lift up the section between the cuts so that it pops up and has a "mountain" fold instead of a "valley" fold.

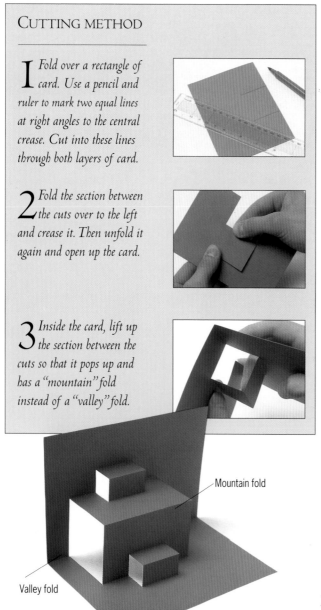

Mountain fold

Valley fold

▲ Practice this simple method and then try cutting out different shaped lines to get different shaped pop-ups.

Central card crease

◀ *If you stick the glued tabs far away from the central card crease, the pop-up shape will stretch flat when you open the card.*
If you stick the glued tabs near to the central card crease, the pop-up shape will point outwards when you open the card.

▶ *Try making more than one shape pop-up in the same card.*
Make one pop-up shape come out of another. Cut out the big shape first, then the little shape.

GLUEING METHOD

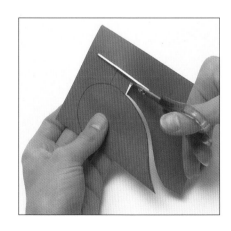

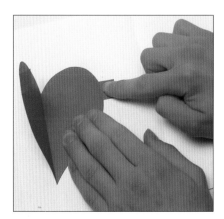

1 Fold round a rectangle of card. Decide what shape you want to pop out. It needs to be symmetrical (the same shape on both sides). Draw this shape on a separate piece of colored paper or card and add a tab to each side.

2 Cut out the shape and fold it in two, making a sharp crease along the middle. Fold the tabs to the back. Then unfold the shape and lay it flat. Run glue down the front of each tab and fold the shape round again (glued tabs outwards).

3 Open the card and lay the pop-up shape down on one side so that a glued tab sticks to the inside of the card. Close the card and press on it so that the other tab will stick to the inside. When you open your card the shape will pop up!

Cards for fun

POP-UPS ARE NOT THE ONLY WAY TO make cards exciting. The cards here are fun to make and also fun to receive. You can make the messages and pictures in them special for the people you are giving them to.

WHAT YOU NEED

....

Sheet of stiff paper
Scraps of plain card
Pencil, ruler, and compass
Sharp scissors and hole punch
Felt-tip pens or paints
Glue and thin glue brush
Paper fastener

ENTER THE SECRET DOORS!

You've really got to search for the secrets inside this card, because it's got doors within doors! You could write a secret message in the final section, or write "Open the birthday doors" on the front and someone's new age deep inside. You could write coded messages on all the doors, and the key to the code inside the last one.

1 *Fold the paper in half widthwise. Fold it in half lengthwise, with a valley fold, then in half again, with a mountain fold.*

2 *Draw a large door on the top sheet. Cut it out and fold it back — make sure you only cut through one layer of paper. Draw two smaller doors inside and do the same. Each time you open a door, draw and cut out another smaller opening on the sheet beneath.*

3 *When you reach the last sheet, stop cutting. Unfold the card carefully to dab a little glue on the corners of each sheet to keep the doors shut. Then fold up the card once more and press down on it firmly to make it stick together.*

▲ *Your finished card can have as many doors as you have folded layers. When you have practiced, try making the doors different shapes.*

CASTLE CARD

Lots of little opening doors and windows reveal hidden faces in this pop-up card. You could put members of your family in the windows – or your pets!

▶ *To make this special card, draw a castle or your own house, cut out flaps for windows, and stick the page onto a piece of backing card. Then draw or paint pictures in the windows.*

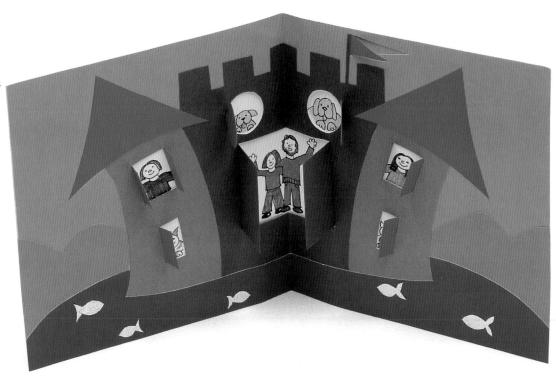

WHIRLING WHEEL

Fix these wheels to the front of a card and write "Happy Birthday" on it. It is based on a traditional card design of over a hundred years ago, when novelty cards of all kinds were very popular.

Turn the wheels to get weird animal combinations!

1 *Fold the card rectangle in half. Open it out again, with the fold pointing toward you as a mountain fold. Measure and mark the middle point on the right side. Use sharp scissors or a punch to make a hole.*

2 *Cut out three card circles – small, medium, and big. Make a hole through the centre of each one. With the smallest one on top, push a paper fastener through each hole and through the middle of the card.*

3 *Open out the paper fastener inside the card – not too tightly or the wheels won't move round. Draw over the card and the circles. Turn the circles round to get different effects.*

◀ *On this card we have drawn animals (you could add the message "Have a wild birthday!"). You could draw human faces on differently decorated presents ("From all your friends"), or monsters ("Have a monster-ous birthday!").*

31

Poster cards

Cards don't have to be small! You can fold thick paper or thin card many times to make a card that opens out to be huge! With a beautiful drawing on it, your friends will want to display it like a poster.

WHAT YOU NEED

Sheet of thin card 16 x 8 inches

Sheet of very thin card or strong paper 16 x 16 inches

Ruler and craft knife, or sharp scissors

Cutting board

Glue and glue brush

Set-square and pencil

Crayons or felt-tips

UNFOLD A SURPRISE!

This card opens out into a big poster for an important, heartfelt message! It relies on careful measuring, scoring, and accurate folding. Try folding some scrap paper first to get the method right before you use more expensive materials.

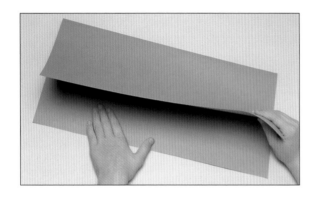

1 Take the paper square. Score and make a mountain fold down the center. Then unfold the paper again.

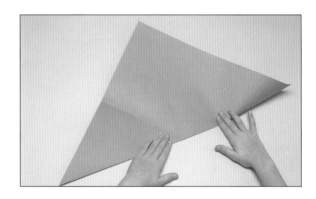

2 Fold diagonally across opposite corners of the paper square to make two valley folds in the shape of an X.

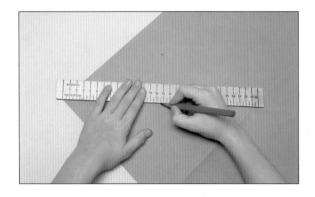

3 Measure 5.75 inches in along the diagonal fold lines, coming from each corner. Mark each spot lightly with a pencil.

4 Use a set square to score a line from this point to the edges of the paper at right angles to the point. Do this on all four corners.

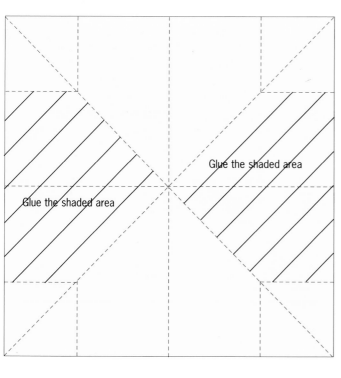

◀ *Glue the back of your folded piece of paper in the areas shown in this diagram. Then stick it onto the folded card rectangle (shown in step 6 below).*

Glue the shaded area

Glue the shaded area

▼ *Draw a big picture on the paper, or write a special message, so it surprises whoever opens it.*

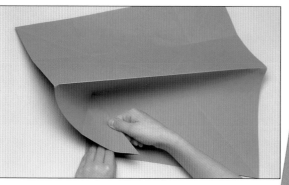

5 Pinch up the corner between the straight lines you have made to change the diagonal valley fold to a mountain fold. Do this on all four corners.

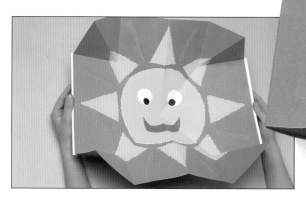

6 Now fold and unfold the card rectangle in half. Press the paper down onto it, lining up the edges and center fold. When you shut your card, make sure the top and bottom of the paper and the corner pieces fold inward.

Paper collages

IF YOU TAKE A LOOK ROUND A greetings card shop, you might see cards that show unusual designs built up from scraps of thin paper, paint, and pieces of typing. This technique is called collage, and you can use it for lots of different effects. A favorite finished collage can be photocopied in color as many times as you like.

▶ *Write or draw on top of the collage paper.*

STRETCHING PAPER

You can make pictures like the ones shown here on a background of card or thick paper. Because glue makes the background quite wet, if you use thin paper you need to stretch it before you use it – that way it will dry flat and smooth, without lumps and bumps. You don't need to stretch card.

WHAT YOU NEED

White watercolor paper
Bowl of water
Brown paper masking tape
(available from
stationery or craft shops)

I Soak the sheet of paper in water for about ten minutes. Lift it out carefully and place it on a flat, clean board. Tape the edges to the board with brown paper masking tape. Wet the back of the masking tape to make it sticky. When dry, the paper can be used for the collage effects shown here. Keep it on the board while you work.

▲ Repeat the same motif in different colors and materials.

TISSUE EXPERIMENTS

Tissue paper is good for making layered pictures because you can partly see through it to the other colors and patterns beneath. Sandwich it with pieces of type, or paint images or words on top. Thick tissue paper is easier to glue down than thin tissue.

1 *Paint a thin layer of PVA glue over the back of each tissue piece. Lay the pieces down flat in the position you want.*

2 *Decorate the tissue by painting patterns or words on top.*

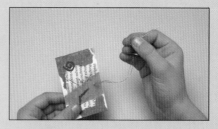

3 *Sew stitches through or try rubbing pastel or wax crayons over the top. Aim for an interesting texture and mix of colors. Words or painted images can give your work a theme, or you can simply use them to get an interesting abstract design.*

Collage frames and mosaics

IT'S POSSIBLE TO DECORATE ALL
kinds of objects using paper
collage pieces. Think carefully about
the colors of the pieces you choose to
put together. Lay them out on paper
first to get the arrangement right.
You can glue on other objects, too,
such as favorite shells, beads, or
autumn leaves. The fun of collages is
in experimenting!

WHAT YOU NEED

....

Piece of thin wood, such as hardboard or ply
Thick paper, such as watercolor paper
Mirror tile
PVA glue and glue brush
Varnish

DECORATIVE MIRROR

You can use collage to decorate wood. You
can make a mirror for your room into a work
of art by decorating a plaque around a mirror
tile with a favorite theme.

1 *Begin by planning
your design and
cutting out the paper
pieces you want. Rub
down the wood with fine
sandpaper and then coat it
with PVA glue.*

2 *Lay the paper pieces
in place, concentrating
on the areas that will
show round the mirror
tile. If they are small it is
easier to place them with
the end of a paintbrush.*

3 *Apply another coat of
PVA over the top,
and leave it to dry
overnight. Then add
another coat and, when
this is dry, add a coat of
varnish. Last, glue on the
mirror tile.*

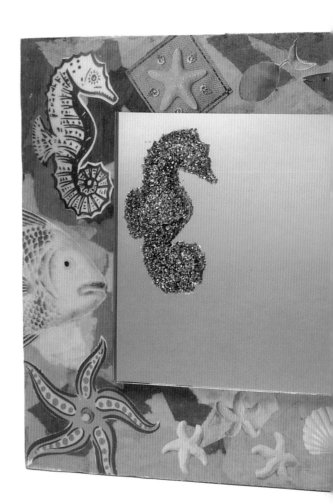

PAPER MOSAIC

In Roman times, mosaics were made from tiny pieces of glass called *tesserae*. You can recreate this look by using paper pieces mounted on thick card or foamboard (a type of card with foam sandwiched in the middle). If you like, work your initials into the design.

▼ *Make a sea-horse for your mirror by cutting out a stencil and laying it on the mirror. Brush a thin layer of glue over the stencil, and remove it. Then scatter glitter over the glued area.*

1 *Before you start on a complicated picture, plan it out first. On a piece of graph paper, color in squares with crayons or felt-tips. This will give you an idea of what the finished mosaic will look like.*

2 *Glue colored paper to foamboard and use your craft knife to cut it evenly into lots of small squares.*

3 *Mix the filler with water to make a thick paste. Spread it, a little at a time, on a square of foamboard. Press the colored squares into the filler, leaving a gap between each one. Leave the mosaic to dry overnight. Coat it with a layer of watered-down PVA and, when this is dry, varnish it.*

Paper weaving

WEAVING IS ONE OF THE SIMPLEST ways to use paper in a decorative way. Weave one color into a contrasting color that shows up well against it. You can use as many different colors as you like. Try weaving different paper textures together, too.

▼ Cut each slit slightly longer than the last to make this corner weaving. It works well on both sides of the paper.

WHAT YOU NEED

....

Colored paper

Ruler

Scissors or craft knife

▶ If you weave into the back of a ready-made envelope, make sure you avoid the glue strip intended for sticking the flap down.

BASIC WEAVING

1 Using a ruler and pencil, lightly draw in a number of vertical cutting lines, evenly spaced. Use a craft knife and ruler to cut along these lines to make slits.

2 Cut strips of colored paper, of equal lengths and wide enough for your design. Dab glue on one end of a strip and secure it to the back of your weaving. Feed it through the slits and secure the other end to the back with glue.

3 Weave all your strips in side by side. If you are weaving through thin paper, you may need to anchor it down as you go. Dab a few spots of glue under the sections between the slits, and flatten them down onto the weaving as you go along.

You needn't be restricted to straight slits. Try cutting them as zigzags or curves. Cut the weaving strips with irregular edges and use black on white or clashing colors

▶ *Make mug coasters by weaving on squares of thick paper, and then covering both sides with clear plastic.*

HANGING HEART

Make this heart to hang on a Christmas tree or as a Valentine's Day gift.

1 *Fold one square in half. Draw half a heart on it and cut round the shape to the fold. Do the same on the other square so you have two hearts.*

2 *On each heart use a craft knife and ruler to cut slits going across. These should be .5 inch apart; do not make them go too near the edge.*

3 *Weave the colored strips through the hearts, starting in the center and working out to the edge. Trim the strips to fit the hearts and glue them in place. Leave both hearts to dry.*

4 *Glue the remaining strip in a loop to the back of one heart. Then glue the two hearts together back to back, hiding the bottom of the loop.*

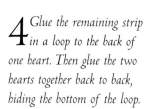

WHAT YOU NEED

Two 4-inch squares of thick paper

Craft knife, ruler, and pencil

Several contrasting-color paper strips 0.5 inch wide and at least 2 .75 inches long.

Glue and glue brush

Colored strip 0.5 inch wide and 4 .75 inches long

▼ *If you like, leave the top of the heart open. You could slip a message inside it. Or use it as a small bag for a wrapped chocolate to give to guests at the end of a meal or a party.*

Woven baskets

PAPER WEAVING TECHNIQUES CAN be applied to 3D objects such as these woven baskets. They are perfect for holding and displaying Easter eggs. Try experimenting by weaving different paper textures to create unusual and eye-catching effects.

WHAT YOU NEED
....
Different colored pieces of medium-thick paper –
you could use ordinary or shiny gift-wrap paper
Ruler, scissors, and pencil
Glue and glue brush
Craft knife and cutting mat

MINI-BASKET

Make mini-baskets and fill them with small Easter eggs in spring, chocolate money at Christmas, or a special present at any time.

1 Choose a colored sheet of paper for the main part of the basket. Measure and draw the diagram opposite and cut the shape out. Then measure and draw a margin 0.5 inch inside, all the way round (shown as a grey line).

2 Measure, mark, and cut slits 0.5 inch apart down the center panel (shown as blue lines on the diagram on the next page). Do the same on the side panels (shown as red lines on the diagram). Cut carefully along all these slits.

3 Cut out lots of 0.5-inch-wide strips for weaving, some long enough for the center panel; some shorter for the side panels. When you have woven them in, glue down the ends.

4 On the wrong side of the basket, score along all the fold lines. Then fold the center panel round and fold the side panels up to meet it. Glue all the flaps inside the basket and leave it to dry.

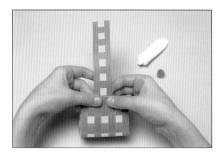

5 Cut a strip of paper 1 x 4.75 inches. Make 0.5-inch-wide slits across it, spacing them 0.5 inch apart. Weave a 0.5-inch-wide strip through the slits to make the basket handle. Glue the ends of the basket handle into the basket.

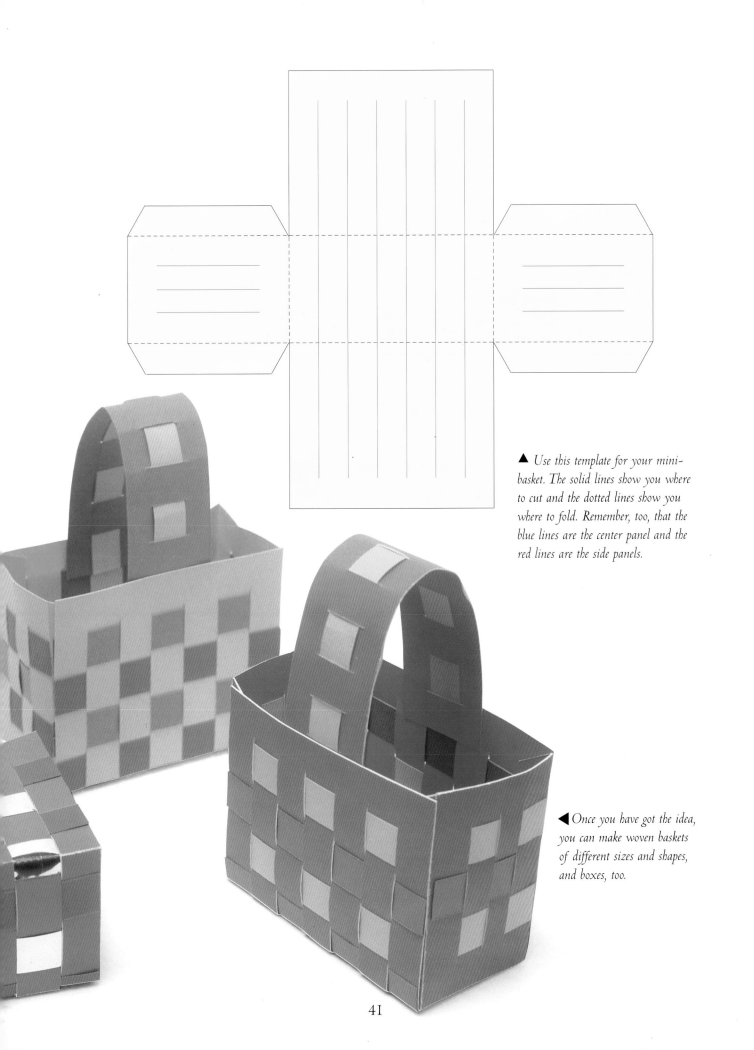

▲ *Use this template for your mini-basket. The solid lines show you where to cut and the dotted lines show you where to fold. Remember, too, that the blue lines are the center panel and the red lines are the side panels.*

◀ *Once you have got the idea, you can make woven baskets of different sizes and shapes, and boxes, too.*

41

Perfect pricking

Pricking is a traditional papercraft in the New England area of the United States. You do it by pricking a series of small holes through paper, then hanging the paper up so that the light shines through the holes from behind, bringing out the pattern.

PRICKING PICTURES

It's best to choose a simple picture or pattern outline to prick. Very detailed, closely worked pricking is hard to see as the holes merge together. You can vary the size of the holes by using needles of different thicknesses. The larger the hole, the more light will shine through.

SAILING BOAT

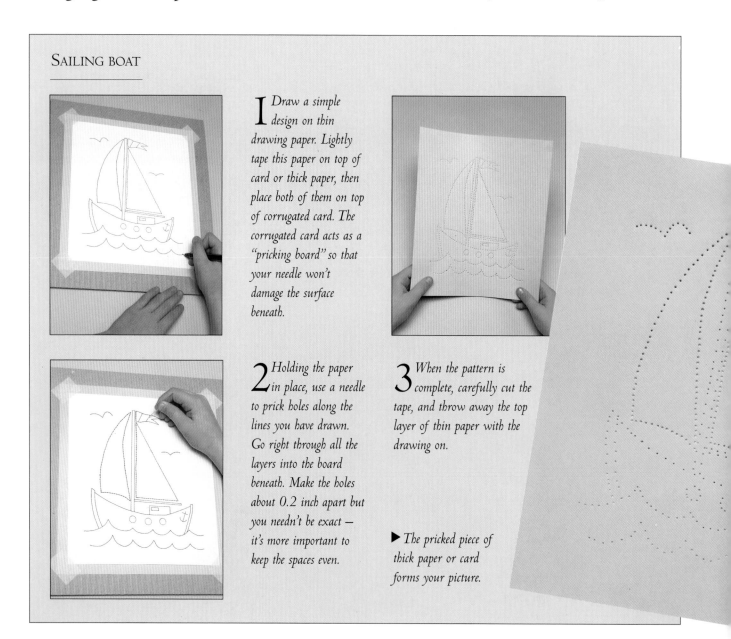

1 Draw a simple design on thin drawing paper. Lightly tape this paper on top of card or thick paper, then place both of them on top of corrugated card. The corrugated card acts as a "pricking board" so that your needle won't damage the surface beneath.

2 Holding the paper in place, use a needle to prick holes along the lines you have drawn. Go right through all the layers into the board beneath. Make the holes about 0.2 inch apart but you needn't be exact — it's more important to keep the spaces even.

3 When the pattern is complete, carefully cut the tape, and throw away the top layer of thin paper with the drawing on.

▶ The pricked piece of thick paper or card forms your picture.

PRICKED FRAME

Why not make a pricked frame, and place your pricked picture inside it? You can make the pattern on the frame pick up the theme of the picture.

WHAT YOU NEED

Thin card or thick paper, cut to size
Thin drawing paper for the pattern, cut to size
Pencil, sticky tape, and scissors
Set of different-sized sewing needles
Scrap piece of corrugated card
Colored tissue paper (optional)

1 *Make a frame, following the instructions on page 19. In this example, the design reflects the sailing boat theme of the main picture.*

▼ *If you glue tissue paper of different colors behind the holes, the light will shine through making lines of different colors.*

2 *Tape your pricked picture behind the frame, but do not add any backing card. Hang it in a window or in front of a lamp, so that the light shines through the holes.*

Toys and games

IN MANY PARTS OF THE WORLD PEOPLE make their own toys and games out of whatever there is to hand. You can do the same using paper and card. It is a lot cheaper than a visit to the toy shop and it provides two activities for the price of one: first you get to make the toy, then you get to play with it!

Paper fastener

◀ *To make the windmill more permanent, punch a hole in the center. Put a paper fastener through the hole and then through a hole in a strip of corrugated thick card. Make sure the windmill can spin freely.*

Drinking straw

WHAT YOU NEED

Two squares of sticky-back paper in contrasting colors

Glue and glue brush

Scissors

Ruler

Drinking straw

Drawing pin

WHIRLY WINDMILL

1 *Stick the two pieces of paper back to back, lining up the edges. Fold the square diagonally to make crease marks in the shape of an X. Measure and cut along each crease from the corner halfway to the center.*

2 *Fold and glue every other point into the center (they will overlap). Push the pin through the center and into the top of the straw. Blow to make the windmill spin round or put it outside for the wind to turn.*

TO PLAY CHANCER

Ask a friend to choose a color from the top of the chancer. Use your fingers to "click" the chancer in and out, one click for each letter of the color your friend has chosen. Then show your friend the inside of the chancer and ask them to choose one of the numbers they can see. Use your fingers to click the chancer that number of times. After they choose another number, look beneath it and read out what you have written underneath. You could write forfeits, and then your friends must do them!

1 Fold the square along its diagonals to make a cross. Then flatten it out again.

2 Take each corner in turn and fold it to the center. Make every fold a sharp crease.

3 Turn the square over and again fold the corners to the center, making the creases sharp.

4 Fold the square in half. Then open this fold and fold the square the other way.

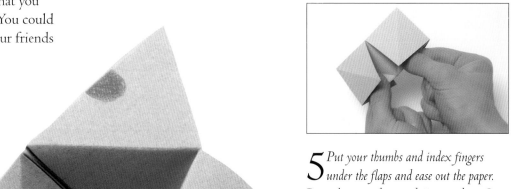

5 Put your thumbs and index fingers under the flaps and ease out the paper. Paint the outer flaps in different colors. Open it up and write numbers inside, up to eight. Write a message underneath each number.

You may be able to move the chancer with one hand, but two is easier!

▶ *You could put nice messages inside the chancer, such as "You are beautiful," or rude ones, such as "You are ugly," or strange ones, such as "You have webbed feet."*

Party table

PAPER DECORATIONS ARE GREAT FOR PARTIES OR festivals. They're inexpensive, and you can enjoy making them. Don't make the patterns too complicated, though, or put in lots of fussy details. Keep the ideas simple and you will achieve a more striking finished look.

NAPKIN FOLDING

Starched linen napkins are really good for holding their shape. They can be folded into very complicated patterns. Here are two simple folded shapes that will work just as well even with paper napkins. Run your finger along all the folds to make the creases sharp.

1 *Unfold a napkin and lay it flat. Fold it diagonally to make a triangle. Fold the outer corners up the middle to make a square.*

2 *Turn the napkin over. Hold the top point in place, and fold it down to make a triangle.*

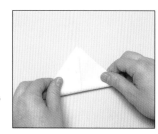

3 *Bend the triangle round and, at the back, tuck one corner inside the folds of the other. Stand the napkin up and gently bend the two loose flaps outwards.*

NAPKIN FOR GLASS

1 *Lay a napkin on the table, folded as a square — a paper one will be already folded this way. Fold the left corner over to the right.*

▲ *Put the napkin in a glass or a paper cup. Gently fan out the edges.*

2 *Take the right corner and fold half the napkin back to the center. Turn the napkin over, and fold the left corner back to the center. Fold the other corners to the center.*

TABLE ACCESSORIES

Start with a plain paper tablecloth and napkins, and stencil designs on them for your own unique theme. Then repeat the image on napkin rings, and place settings made from rectangles or round circles of card. You could even use the same stencil for your party invitations, too.

1 *Draw a design onto the stencilling card and cut round it carefully, using a craft knife. Keep the design simple so that you can cut it accurately.*

2 *Place the stencil on a napkin. Load your brush or sponge with a little paint or oil-based crayon. Then dab it through the stencil onto the napkin. When the paint is dry, gently lift off the card so that you can use it again.*

▲ *Use your stencil to decorate a whole range of party goods with a unified theme. You can vary the colors on different things.*

NAPKIN RINGS

Make napkin rings to carry through your party table theme. Start with basic rings and decorate them by sticking on objects or paper shapes. You could even glue on small origami shapes (see pages 84–87).

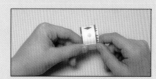

1 *First decorate the strip by shaping the edges with scissors, painting it, or sticking colored paper onto it. Curve the strip round, and glue or tape it at the back to make a ring.*

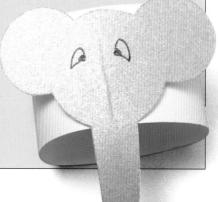

Party decorations

Whether you are having a few friends round informally, or doing something a bit more special, individually made decorations will make your party really swing!

TEDDY-IN-THE BOX SETTING CARDS

Make each guest a personalized table setting card that will follow your overall theme. Here are two ideas that you can easily adapt to make new images.

Write the name of each guest on the front of the cards.

Teddy pops up

1 *Score and fold a card rectangle in half across the narrow middle. Lay it flat again and draw a teddy shape coming up from the middle line made by the fold.*

2 *Decorate the teddy and the "box" beneath him. Carefully cut round the teddy shape above the card. Then fold the card back down again so the teddy stands up.*

DINNER DRESS CARD

1 *Score and fold a card rectangle in half across the narrow middle. Decorate each card with a white shirt and collar.*

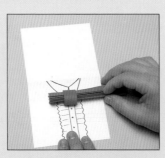

2 *Glue a loop of colored paper near the top of the shirt. Make fan folds out of a strip of colored paper. Feed the folded paper through the loop.*

PARTY PAPER CHAINS

Decorate the party room with your own unique paper chains. Here are a few ideas to try.

WHAT YOU NEED

Colored string or cord
Colored tissue paper rectangles
for bow chain
Colored thin paper strips for cut-out chain

CUT-OUT CHAIN

1 *Fold a strip of paper back and forth concertina-style (see pages 12–14). Draw a shape on the front, making sure that the shape runs over both edges of the paper.*

2 *Cut round the shape through all the paper layers. Do not cut along any folds. This is so that all the individual shapes are still joined when the chain is opened.*

3 *When the strip is opened up, it makes a chain. If you want, join several chains together.*

▶ *Do not cut over the folds when you are cutting out the shapes or the banner will come apart. Try making them from different kinds of paper for different effects. Shiny paper chains looks great swinging from the walls and ceiling!*

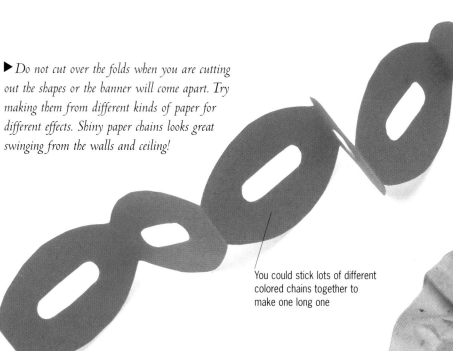

You could stick lots of different colored chains together to make one long one

▶ *To make a chain of bows, put a length of colored string round the middle of bunched-up rectangles of tissue paper. Fan out the rectangles to look like bows.*

Boxes and bags

Aideal way to make a gift extra-
special. Use thick, flexible paper to
make a bag, and find thin, bendy
card to make a box. Decorate your
gift containers in themes related to
the present inside.

WHAT YOU NEED

Plastic drinks bottle
Sharp scissors
Ruler, tape measure, and felt-tip pen
Heavy wrapping paper or thin card
Glue and glue brush
Decorative tissue or cellophane
Ribbon

GIFT BASKET BOX

Here's an easy way to make a gift container using
paper, and the method has the added benefit of
recycling old packaging, too!

*1 Use a ruler and felt-tip
to measure up from the
bottom of the drinks bottle.
Mark a line round the bottle
as high as you want your bag
to be, and cut round it.*

*2 Measure the base of the
bottle, and up from the
base. Cut a strip of card or
paper about 1 inch higher and
1 inch longer than the
container.*

*3 Put glue round the
outside of the container
and along one narrow edge of
the paper strip. Wrap the strip
round the container and glue
the overlapping edge firmly at
the back.*

*4 Put some crumpled tissue
or cellophane in the
bottom to cushion your gift,
and more round it to cover it
up. Then tie a pretty ribbon
round the whole box.*

50

BASIC BAG

Once you've made a gift bag, wrap your present loosely in tissue and put it inside. This template shows measurements for a medium-sized bag. If you want a bigger or smaller one, make sure you alter all the dimensions equally.

1 *Use a pencil and ruler to draw this bag design on the back of the paper. Score lightly along all the black dotted lines. Fold inwards all the lines you have scored.*

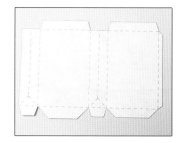

2 *Turn over and score along the red dotted lines. Fold them in and then flatten them again. Then turn over again and glue down the tabs along the top edge (this makes the bag extra-strong).*

3 *Glue together the tabs underneath. Then glue the side of the bag together and hold it until it dries. Gently pinch the sides of the bag along the lines you scored and folded.*

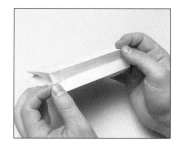

4 *Pinch the top of the bag together, and punch through it to make two sets of holes on either side. Thread a length of ribbon through each set of holes, and knot the ends inside the bag.*

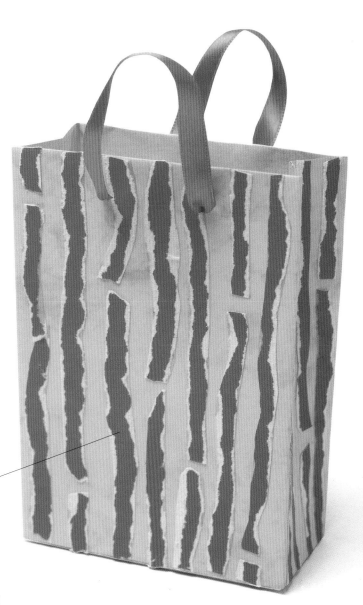

This bag is decorated with collage strips to match the ribbon handles

Storage boxes

A STURDY BOX WITH A LID MAKES an ideal toy box or container for a collection. It can be made in any size using a simple template, and decorated to suit its contents. A decorated box is also an ideal way to present a gift to someone.

BOX WITH LID

Here is a simple box with its own separate lid. You can make several smaller ones to fit inside.

1 *Score along the lines. Fold them all inward and then flatten them out again. Fold the box up as shown.*

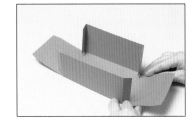

2 *Dab glue along the narrow side edges, and fold the box up again. Hold the edges together firmly while the glue dries.*

3 *Brush glue along the inside of the two top narrow edges. Fold them to the inside, and hold them in place until the glue dries.*

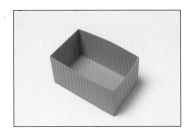

Cut along the solid lines; fold along the broken lines.

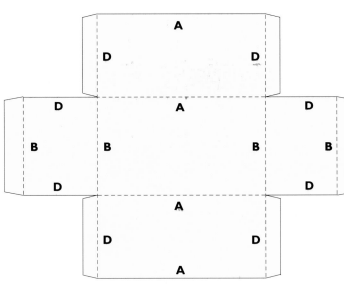

▲ *To make the box, copy template A onto the back of the card. Make it any overall size you like, but make sure that measurements that have the same letter are the same as each other.*

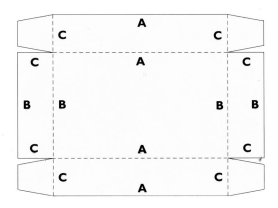

▲ *To make the lid, use template B. Fold up and glue the lid in the same way as the box. Wait until it is dry before you put it on your box.*

52

◀ To give your box a frill, cut strips of crepe paper twice the depth of the lid. Paste glue round the inside of the lid and press the crepe paper onto it, gathering up the crepe paper into pleats as you do so.

▶ This box has two more boxes inside, each one made slightly smaller than the last. They all match, and open up a bit like a set of Russian dolls.

◀ This box was made out of card with a pattern cut in the sides before it was folded up. Contrasting colored paper was stuck on the inside edges so it shows through the holes.

Papier mache molds

PAPIER MACHE IS A GREAT WAY TO RECYCLE paper. Newspaper, computer printout paper, cartridge paper, and even tissue and crepe paper are all suitable. There are several different methods. Start with layering and, if you enjoy this, go on to work with pulp.

WHAT YOU NEED

Balloon and thread

Bowl (for mixing)

Wallpaper paste (containing a fungicide), mixed with water to a creamy consistency

Paper torn up into small squares

Paintbrushes

Apron and newspaper (to protect clothes and table)

Craft knife or sharp scissors

White water-based paint

Paints to decorate

LAYERING A BALLOON MASK

Laying strips of paper on top of each other around a mold makes a strong paper crust. The most important rule is to let the paper dry between layers, and so this method takes a few days to complete. The steps below show how to make a mask using a balloon as a mold.

1 *Hang up the balloon with the thread. Soak paper squares in the paste, then lay them overlapping on the balloon until it is covered. Immediately add a second layer.*

2 *Let the pasted paper dry for several hours. Then add two more layers, and let it dry again. Put on six to eight layers in total, letting it dry every two layers.*

▶ *When the undercoat is dry, decorate your mask, making holes for the eyes and mouth. Then varnish it two or three times to protect it.*

3 *Pop the balloon by sticking a long needle right through the paper. Then cut the shape in half to make an oval. Paint it with white water-based paint, and let it dry.*

▶ *This "fire" mask was made by cutting out a card template (see page 74) with the top cut to look like flames. You can then use layers of papier mâché to alter the surface texture of the mask — for example, to give a raised outline to the eye holes and the outside edge.*

MAKING A BOWL

You can layer papier mache onto lots of different molds, and they needn't cost anything. Here we show you how to make a bowl using another bowl as a mold. To remove the mold easily after your work is dry, before applying the papier mache either cover the mold with a layer of petroleum jelly, or wrap it in a smooth layer of plastic film.

1 *Soak the paper squares in the paste, and cover the mold with petroleum jelly or plastic film. Lay the paper over the mold until it is covered.*

2 *When the mold is completely covered, paint a thick layer of thinned wallpaper paste or PVA all over it. Repeat with more paper and glue twice more. Leave the mold to dry for 24 hours in a warm place.*

5 *When the decorations are finished and completely dry, paint two or three layers of varnish over the entire bowl, inside and outside, to protect it.*

3 *Remove the papier mâché shape carefully from the mold. Trim any rough edges carefully with scissors. Then rub it gently all over with fine sandpaper to smooth it, and paint it with undercoat.*

4 *Cut a piece of decorative colored paper to fit the bottom of the bowl. Paint a thin layer of paste in the bottom of the bowl, and press the paper onto it gently. Cut circles of colored tissue paper to decorate the sides.*

Choose the colors for decorating your bowl to fit in with what you plan to put in it.

Papier mache models

ONCE YOU HAVE MADE A FEW PAPIER MACHE items using simple molds that you remove, try following the steps here to make more complicated things, such as animals. First you have to make the basic shape, called an armature. Start with a simple one!

WHAT YOU NEED

Cardboard tubes from toilet rolls and kitchen rolls, for the tail, neck, ears, and legs

Carboard oblong box with a lid, such as a shoe box

Smaller oblong box for the head

Scissors, glue, and sticky tape

Papier mâché for layering

ANIMAL MODEL

In Japan, papier mache replicas of animals are thought to ward off evil spirits. Make your own by layering onto a cardboard body base, or armature. An armature, unlike a mold, is not removed when the model is dry.

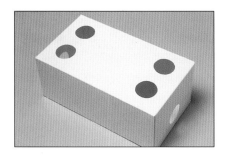

1 *Plan out your animal armature before you start. Make holes in the main body box where you want to stick tubes in.*

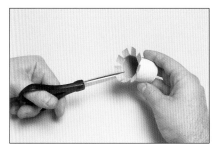

2 *To make the leg tubes, use a tube of paper and snip about 0.25 inch into one end, evenly all round with 0.25-inch gaps. Fan out these tabs. Measure four tubes so that you get the legs all the same length.*

3 *The tail tube needs to be at an angle. Snip into the tube deeper on one side, to make tabs that are longer on one side than on the other.*

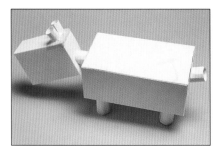

4 *Glue the tabs of the leg and tail tubes inside the holes on the main body. Then make more tubes for the neck, join it at an angle to a smaller box for the head, and add the ears.*

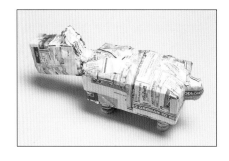

5 *Once your animal body is constructed, layer papier mâché onto it. Add several layers for strength and let them dry completely.*

6 *When your animal is quite dry, paint on a thick layer of undercoat. Afterwards, decorate it as you like, and finally varnish it. Handle it with care when you work.*

PAPIER MACHE TEDDY BEAR

Once you have learned the simple technique of using an armature, you can apply it to a whole range of other animals, for example this teddy bear (see right). Create an armature for the teddy bear using toilet rolls for the body and limbs, and a ball or other round object for the head. Build up the ears using the layering technique.

▶ *Once the layers have dried, paint a beige base color over the entire bear. Use white for the feet and hands and then add the mouth and eye detail in black.*

Studded collar

Painted on eyes and nose

▲ *The dog collar is made from a thin strip of textured card, with gold studs made from round pieces of gold paper. You could make the studs raised by cutting a line from the edge to the center, overlapping one edge over the other, and sticking them to make a shallow cone (see page 25).*

Stationery shop

STATIONERY DOESN'T HAVE TO BE BORING! HERE ARE some suggestions for making unusual envelopes and writing paper for special occasions. Try these two ways to make your very own stationery storage folders. They're ideal for keeping paper scraps and examples of artwork, too.

WHAT YOU NEED

A big piece of stiff paper
or thin card

Glue and glue brush

Ruler and pencil

Scissors

Sticky tape

Length of tape

LACE-UP WALLET

Use the template shown on the right to make a special wallet. You don't have to make it the size shown here, as long as all the sides that have the same letters are the same length. For example, all the sides marked A could be 20 inches and all those marked B could be 10 inches.

1 *Using a ruler, draw the wallet as shown in the diagram (far right). Cut out this shape and score the lines.*

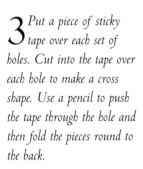

2 *Cut holes where shown. Cut the edges into a wavy shape if you like. Fold in the left and right sides. Fold up the bottom edge, and glue it on top of the left and right sides.*

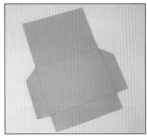

3 *Put a piece of sticky tape over each set of holes. Cut into the tape over each hole to make a cross shape. Use a pencil to push the tape through the hole and then fold the pieces round to the back.*

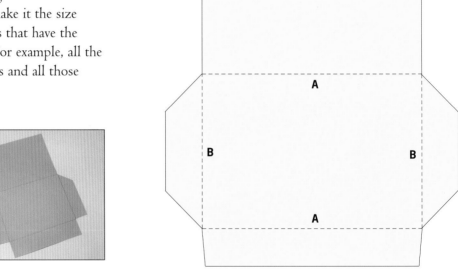

Cut along the solid lines; fold along the broken lines.

▼ *To close the wallet, lace the string through the bottom set of holes, then up through the top set. Tie a bow.*

TWO KINDS OF ENVELOPE

You can make good envelopes out of medium-thickness paper. Make them any size you like, by scaling the measurements shown here up or down. Score the lines and fold the envelopes as shown.

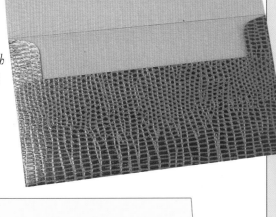

▶ *Envelope with a straight-edged flap.*

◀ *This envelope has a V-shaped flap.*

DECORATING ENVELOPES

▶ *Glue thin wrapping paper to one side of the paper before you cut the envelope out. Fold the envelope with the wrapping paper inside.*

▶ *Glue thin wrapping paper to one side of the paper before you cut the envelope out. This time, fold the envelope with the wrapping paper outside, and glue on an address and stamp label if you want to mail your work.*

▶ *Stick on torn pieces of brightly colored tissue paper to line a pre-made envelope. If you stick on pieces of cut paper, position them away from the fold line.*

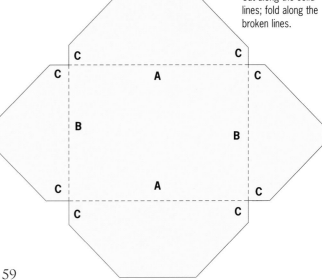

Cut along the solid lines; fold along the broken lines.

Personal stationery

WHAT YOU NEED
....
Writing paper
Sponge
Craft knife
Water-based paint
Kitchen paper

As well as making your own writing paper, cards, and envelopes, you can decorate them – or ready-bought stationery – in a way that makes them uniquely yours. Put your own initials on them, or add pictures special to you – showing your hobbies, perhaps, or illustrating something in your letter.

PRINTING

1 Make a printing block with a piece of thin sponge – look for thin, sponge-backed pan cleaners in the supermarket. Cut out a simple shape, such as the initial letter of your name.

2 Mix water-based paint on a flat plate – choose a pale color that you will be able to write over. Dab the sponge into the paint and then onto some kitchen paper to get rid of any excess. Then push it down onto the writing paper as often as you like.

▼ You can decorate just the margins of your paper, or all over it provided that the stamps are light enough for you to write over. Then you could make envelopes to match.

Cut as many initial letters as you like – why not make decorated paper as presents for your friends?

PICTURE TAB PAPER

Here's an easy but clever way to make an unusual letterhead for the top of a special letter. When the right-hand tab is pulled, a new picture appears! You could write words or draw pictures on the hidden part.

1 Measure and draw two 1-inch long slits near the top of the paper as shown. Cut carefully along the slits with a craft knife.

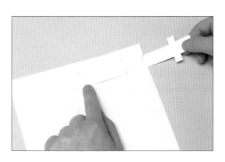

2 Cut the thick paper into a strip with tabs, as shown. Thread it through the slits, with the end underneath.

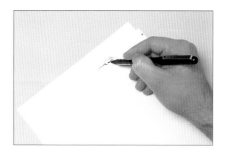

3 Push the strip in as far as it will go. Draw a picture or write a message on the part of the strip that shows.

4 Pull the tab out a little and draw another picture on the new section that is revealed. Then push the tab back into position.

▶ *You can make as many threaded strips as you like, but don't put them too close together or your writing paper may tear.*

Tissue flowers

TISSUE PAPER IS TRANSLUCENT, WHICH means it is thin enough for light to shine through. That gives it a delicate, glowing quality that you can use to good effect in papercraft designs. It's cheap to buy and comes in lots of bright colors.

WHAT YOU NEED

Colored tissue paper
Scissors and sticky tape
Air ball or a ball of oasis
Piece of thin dowelling or an old pencil
Flower pot full of sand
Ribbon for decoration

TOPIARY FLOWER TREE

These flowers made from balls of tissue make a pretty table decoration. Use an air ball to anchor a small version, and a florist's oasis if you want to make a larger one — see the tip below for what these are.

1 *If you have an oasis, use a pencil to poke holes in it. Then push dowelling or the pencil up into the oasis or air ball. Cut a long strip of tissue and wrap it round the stick. Tape it in place at the top and bottom.*

2 *Cut out tissue circles about 5 inches in diameter. You can do this quickly by drawing round the edge of a plate as a template, and cutting through several layers together. Fold each circle in half, in half again and then in half again. Twist the end.*

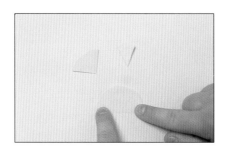

3 *If you use an air ball, glue round the holes first. Then push a tissue piece into each hole. Fluff out the tissue to cover up the ball or oasis. Add more until the ball is covered.*

4 *Stick the dowelling or pencil firmly down into the flower pot of sand and tie some ribbon round the top for decoration.*

ANCHORING THE FLOWER

An air ball (a practice golf ball) is made of plastic with holes in. An oasis (used by florists for flower arranging) is a type of spongy foam ideal for sticking delicate things in.

TISSUE ROSES

Glue these roses onto hats, masks, fancy dress costumes, and gift boxes.

WHAT YOU NEED

Scissors and pencil
Glue and gluebrush
Good-quality tissue paper
Sticky tape

1 *Cut out two small tissue circles (use a cup as a template if you like). Cut out two medium-sized ones and two larger ones. Lay the circles on top of each other with the biggest at the bottom.*

2 *Twist them together underneath the center, so that they bunch together like petals, and gently spread them out. Wrap a small piece of tape around the twist to hold them in place.*

PARTY STICKS

Make these party sticks out of brightly colored paper and strong straws. Stick them in ice-cream sundaes as decoration.

1 *Fold a sheet of tissue until it is about 3 inches wide, with about ten layers on top of each other; if it is pre-folded, don't unfold it. Cut a section 4 inches from the top.*

2 *Glue one edge of the section to the top of a stick, with about 2.5 inches poking up above the stick. Wind the tissue round and round. Glue the other edge in place.*

WHAT YOU NEED

Sheets of tissue, folded if possible
Glue and glue brush
Some thin dowelling sticks

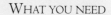

3 *Cut down into the tissue to make a fringe. Push your finger down into the middle to spread the fringe outwards.*

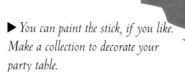

▶ *You can paint the stick, if you like. Make a collection to decorate your party table.*

Puppets and kites

THERE'S NO END TO THE TOYS YOU CAN MAKE with paper. Here we show you how to make shadow puppets, and a clever kite that fills with air when you run with it. Try inventing your own shapes and patterns for both of these!

SHADOW PUPPETS

Shadow puppets are traditional in parts of Asia. You can make your own versions in card and tissue paper with a screen to perform behind. Or you can simply hold your puppet up to a window or a lamp so that the light shines through it.

1 *Draw a shape onto the card. Cut round the outline and cut out smaller shapes from the middle. Don't go too near the edge.*

2 *Brush glue over the back of the animal. Stick tissue on so that it shows through the holes. Trim off any edges that show round the outside.*

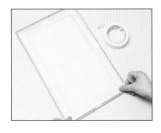

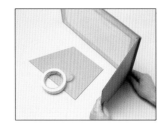

3 *To make a puppet screen, cut out one side of a cardboard box. Cut out the middle to make a frame. Tape a piece of greaseproof paper to the back over the hole.*

4 *Cut two side pieces from the box, and tape them to the back of your screen as shown, to make it stand up. The tops of the supports should slope downwards.*

5 *Place the screen near the edge of a table. Place a lamp behind the table, so it shines directly through the screen from behind. To perform with your puppets, tape or glue plant sticks to the backs so you can hold them from beneath. Sit your audience in front of the screen. Close the curtains and turn off all lights. Then switch on the lamp, and move your puppets behind the screen.*

CARP KITE

Every year in Japan, there is a kite festival for children to fly their home-made carp kites. The carp fish traditionally represents strength. Make your own version and hang it up as a decoration when you're not flying it.

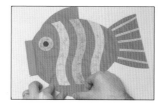

1 *Cut out two carp shapes from tissue paper. You can use the big one on this page to help you. Stick on tissue eyes, body stripes, and fins.*

2 *Turn them over. Cut two strips of card 2 inches wide. Glue a strip along the edge of each mouth, on the wrong side. Trim the card to match the mouth edges. Leave them to dry thoroughly.*

3 *Run a very thin line of glue round the inside of one body shape but not along the mouth, which will stay open. Lay one fish body on top of the other and gently press along the glued edges. Leave them to dry.*

4 *Thread the needle with cotton and knot one end. Thread it out through the card in the middle of a mouth. Thread it round and back through the other mouth to make a loop. Or, if you prefer, tape the thread in place.*

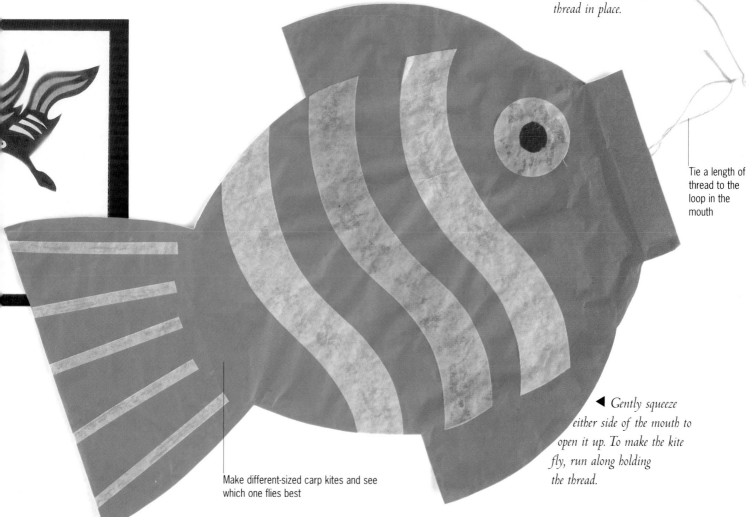

Tie a length of thread to the loop in the mouth

Make different-sized carp kites and see which one flies best

◀ *Gently squeeze either side of the mouth to open it up. To make the kite fly, run along holding the thread.*

Handy hats

MAKE A FASHION HAT YOU CAN really wear, or a zany fancy-dress hat for wild parties. The hats on the right are made from basic paper shapes. They can be personalized by adding your own decorations.

CONE HATS

A basic cone shape is very adaptable. By making a tall or a flattish cone, you can get different-looking hat designs.

Add a rim (see page 68) to make a wizard's hat

1 *Lay the paper rectangle on a flat surface. Starting at the bottom right corner, roll it up into a cone shape — the point will be in the top right corner.*

2 *Holding the cone together, try it on your head for size and adjust it until it fits. To hold the cone in place, tape along the loose edge on the outside and along the loose edge inside.*

3 *Draw a pencil line round the bottom of the cone to make a level edge — if you need to, use a ruler to get it even all round. Cut round the line.*

▶ *To make a princess' hat, attach strips of tissue paper or crepe paper to the pointed end of the hat.*

▶ *This party hat is made from a shorter, flatter cone decorated with paper scraps.*

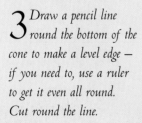

CHINESE HAT

This style of flat cone hat is traditional among workers in China. It is excellent for providing shade from the sun.

WHAT YOU NEED

Piece of stiff paper or thin card, at least 20 x 20 inches

Something round to use as a template, with a diameter of 16–20 inches

Pencil, sticky tape, ruler

Materials for decoration

Cord or string

1 *Place the round shape on the paper and draw round it. Cut out the circle. Use a ruler to find the center of the circle. Draw a line from the center to the edge and cut along this line.*

2 *Bring one edge round to overlap the other, to make a shallow cone. Tape the edges together. Tape two lengths of string opposite each other inside the hat. Tie them round your chin to keep the hat on.*

▼ *Make a hat from thin but strong paper. Thread wool through a large darning needle and sew it in big stitches round the bottom of the hat.*

Plaited ribbon

▶ *Chinese hats were popular fashion items in the 1950s. Get "the look" by adding a big tissue or crepe paper bow to the back of your hat (see page 72). Or spiral a piece of rope, curtain cord, or plaited ribbon down from the top.*

▶ *Roll up and twist lengths of crepe paper and glue them round a hat, spiralling down from the top.*

67

Fancy dress hats

ONE SURE WAY TO GET YOURSELF noticed at a party is to wear a stunning hat of your own make. Adapt the examples shown here by coloring or decorating them.

HEADBAND HAT

You can make many hats that look very different by using simple paper headbands.

1 Cut a strip of card 2.5 inches wide and 3 inches longer than the measurement round your head. Put the two ends together, overlapping by 1.5 inches, check the fit and tape them together.

2 Glue the band to the bottom of a hat – here, a silver band, decorated with scrunched-up sweet papers, is attached to a piece of gold card with spikes cut out of the top to make a crown.

RIMMED HAT

Add rims to top hats, cowboy hats – anything!

1 Make the top part of a hat (either a cone or a wide band). Lay it on top of another, bigger piece of card, and draw a wider circle around the base.

2 Use a ruler to find and mark the center of the circle. With a pencil and compass, draw another circle about 1 inch inside the first one.

3 Cut round the inner circle. Snip from the inner edge to the line of the other circle to make tabs that you can push up. Put the hat top over the tabs, and glue the two together.

▼ Feather shapes from colored paper, glued to a decorated headband, make a Native American headdress.

◄ Two rabbit ears made of gray card with pink insides complete a rabbit headband.

SUN CAP

Make this basic sun-cap shape and personalize it by changing the brim.

WHAT YOU NEED

Piece of stiff paper 9.5 x 12.5 inches

Sharp scissors, or craft knife and cutting board

Pencil, ruler, and compass

Tape measure

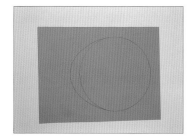

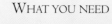

1 *Measure round your head and draw a circle this size at one end of the card rectangle. Using your pencil, make the circle into an oval as shown.*

2 *Inside the oval, measure and draw lines 0.5 inches apart. Cut along the lines to the edge of the oval.*

3 *Round off the corners of the rectangle and push the oval partly down onto your head with the brim at the front. If the hat is too small, cut the lines a little longer towards the front.*

◀ *To make the top of the hat, glue in a circle of crepe paper, or make a circle of card with tabs round the outside. Glue the tabs into the hat.*

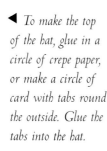

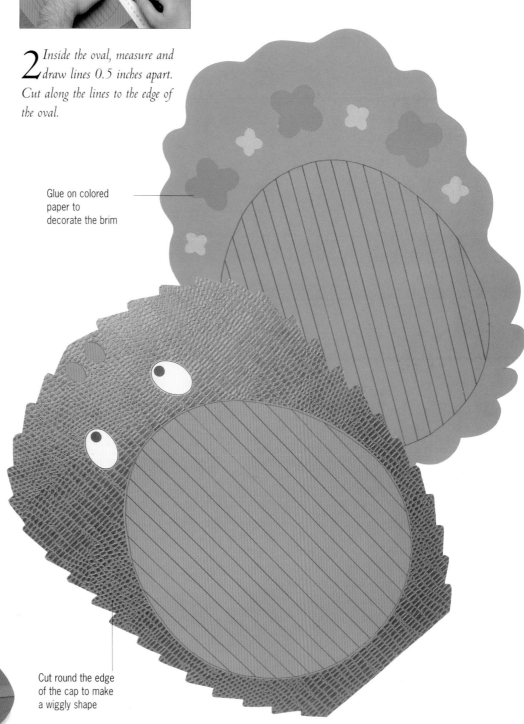

Glue on colored paper to decorate the brim

Cut round the edge of the cap to make a wiggly shape

Fancy dress clothes

Next time you want a fancy dress for a party, you won't need to hire an expensive costume – instead, you can make one of these outfits all on your own using papercraft skills. Ask your friends to help you, and it will be even more fun!

What you need

Rolls of different-colored crepe paper
Tape measure and pencil or felt-tip pen
Glue and gluebrush
Two colored paper strips 18 x 1.5 inches
Scissors

Tube dress

This basic crepe paper dress can be adapted for a variety of different looks.

1 *First take your measurements: round your bottom plus 6 inches for the width, and from under your arm to just above your knee for the length. Cut out a rectangle of crepe paper. Put glue down one edge and bring the two edges together to make a tube, overlapping the glued edge by 2 inches.*

2 *Wriggle into the tube. Get a friend to help you fit the narrow strips over your shoulders from front to back, to make straps. Get them to mark where the straps meet the front and back, and how long they should be. Then take off the tube and glue the straps in place.*

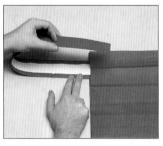

3 *Using different-colored crepe paper, cut some strips about 4 inches deep, and the same width as the tube. Cut almost up to the edge to make a fringe, then put glue along the uncut edge, and glue the fringe to the tube dress. Make as many fringes as you like.*

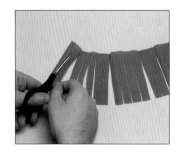

This headband is made from silver card with a feather shape and a big star.

A fringe has been added around the top of the dress.

◄ *This Native American dress is decorated with stars.*

The hem of the dress is fringed, and two contrasting fringes have also been added on.

CAVEMAN OUTFIT

Cut a rectangle of brown crepe paper and, before making a tube dress, cut the top and bottom edges so they look ragged. Stick on some patches of colored paper and draw felt-tip stitching round these.

The club is made from a kitchen paper tube covered with brown crepe paper, with a rolled-up ball of crepe paper stuck on the end.

TWENTIES DRESS

Make a short tube dress out of brightly colored paper, with a paper fringe on the hem in a contrasting color. Then add lots of squares of crepe paper, glued to the hem of the dress, to make an uneven hemline. You can even make a paper "boa" to complete your outfit (see right)!

PAPER BOA

Feather boas were worn by all the "flappers" in the Twenties. Here's an idea for one made out of paper.

WHAT YOU NEED

50 squares of crepe paper 12 x 12 inches, or a box of square tissues
Strong thread 39 inches long
Sewing needle

1 *Lay each square flat and pick it up in the middle. It will fold into an arrow shape. Gently twist round the top.*

2 *Thread the needle and make a knot in one end. Then thread through the top of each arrow shape. Push the paper down, so it bunches and sticks out in different directions.*

3 *When you have finished, tie another knot in the end of the thread. Puff out the paper so the boa looks good.*

Shirts and waistcoats

Here is some more wild and whacky paper clothing to try out. If you do it well, no one will guess what your stylish designer gear is really made of, but don't go out in the rain!

Paper bow tie

Make bow ties as bright as you like! Wear them for fun with your ordinary clothes, or as part of fancy dress.

1 *Cut a piece of crepe paper 6.25 x 13.75 inches. Fold the two ends in to the center. Glue or tape them down, with one edge overlapping the other.*

2 *Cut the elastic to the measurement of your neck plus 4.75 inches, and knot the two ends together. Scrunch up the middle of the tie and glue the knot to the back.*

3 *Cut a strip of paper 1.25 x 2.5 inches, and wrap it round the middle, taping it in place at the back. Fan out the tie on either side.*

Waistcoat

Make a fancy dress waistcoat to go with your tie! You could add a sheriff's badge for a cowboy waistcoat, or fancy buttons and a lace collar.

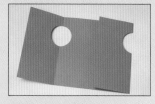

1 *Cut the paper to your size. Fold the two ends into the middle. Cut out an arm circle on each fold 2 inches from the top.*

2 *Turn down the corners to make a collar. Pockets, buttons, or badges make good decorations for your waistcoat.*

Decorate your tie with pieces of paper in a contrasting color

Fancy buttons

Badge

FALSE SHIRT

Fool your friends with this fake shirt! Tie it round your neck
and waist, and then button up a jacket or cardigan over the
top so that nobody can see the edges.

WHAT YOU NEED

Stiff paper

Ruler, pencil, and tape measure

Scissors

Four pieces of string, 12 inches long,
knotted at one end

Hole punch

Colored paper pieces to glue on
for decoration

1 *Cut the paper into the
shape using your body
measurements. In the middle
at the top cut out a curve for
your neck.*

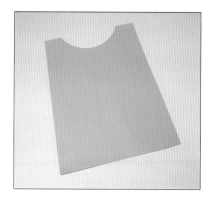

2 *Round off the corners.
Punch holes in the sides
and the shoulders, and thread
a length of string through each
hole. Decorate your shirt
however you like. Then tie the
top strings behind your neck,
and the bottom strings round
your waist.*

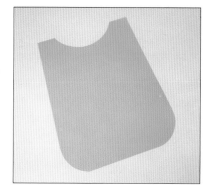

▲ *This fake dress shirt has a white paper collar, shirt
frill, and black bow tie. The frill is made from a length
of lace.*

◀ *This clown's shirt has a ruff made from a circle of
crepe paper. Cut a line from the side to the middle and
concertina-fold the circle. Then open it out and glue the
edges to the shirt. Decorate the shirt with paper shapes.*

73

Mask magic

Masks are the perfect way to dress up a party costume, and you can really let your imagination go. Better still, invite your friends round for a mask-making day – provide materials such as glue and card, and you can all make your own unique masks!

WHAT YOU NEED

Scrap paper and stiff paper or thin card
Scissors, pencil, and tape measure
Glue and glue brush
Stiff straw, plant stick, or length of elastic
Paint or paper pieces for decoration

EYE MASK

This is one of the easiest masks to make, so it's probably a good one to start with. You can decorate it in lots of different ways.

1 *Practice first by cutting a rectangle of scrap paper 7 x 3 inches. Fold it in half to make a shape 3.5 x 3 inches. On one side draw a round shape up to the fold.*

2 *Cut out the outline shape. Then unfold the paper, and hold it up to your face to check the size. Mark where the eyes should be, and cut them out.*

3 *Once you are happy with the size and eye positions on your practice mask, use it as a template to cut out a mask from stiff paper. Decorate this with paints or glued-on paper shapes.*

4 *Punch a hole in each side, thread some elastic through, and tie the mask round your head. Alternately, tape a stick to one side, so that you can hold the mask up to your eyes.*

Pointed ends look good

You could cut the outline as a wavy zigzag

Make a mask in a heart shape

▲ *Make eye masks more elaborate by glueing on card hats and hair. Paint the eye mask skin color and draw eyebrows and eyelashes on.*

VENETIAN FIREBIRD MASK

This traditional design is worn at the spring carnival in Venice that takes place every year in the week of Mardi Gras.

1 Fold the card triangle in half lengthwise. Fold back two corners on the nose section of your eye mask.

▼ *For an authentic Venetian mask, stick three or four layers of papier mâché pieces over the card before you paint it (see page 54). You could pinch up the papier mache to make a raised edge around the eyes.*

2 Put the nose over the eye mask, and tape or glue the two corners inside the nose to keep it in place.

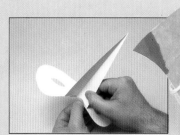

More amazing masks

Masks are popular the world over at festivals and celebration times. Look in the library for books on different countries to get some extra ideas for decorating the basic masks shown here.

What you need

....

Stiff paper or thin card, 7 x 8 inches

Scissors

Elastic or string

Paints and anything else you like for decoration

Hole punch

Full face masks

This mask covers your whole face. You can adapt it to any theme you like.

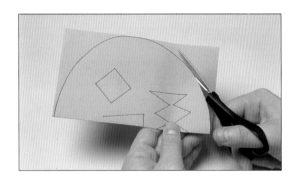

1 *Fold the paper in half lengthwise. Draw half an oval, an eye, half a mouth, and half a nose shape. Cut round the shapes you have drawn and open up your mask.*

2 *Punch a hole on either side, just above where your ears will be. Knot elastic or string lengths through the holes so you can tie them round your head.*

▲ *This Neptune mask has different lengths of green and blue paper making a beard and hair. Paper fish are glued into the beard.*

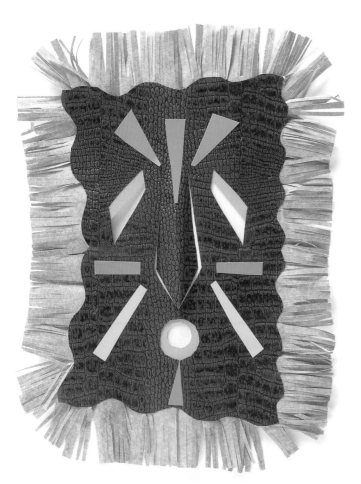

▲ *For African dance masks, cut out different shapes like these.*

▲ *For a traditional ancient Greek theater mask, cut out a shape with pointed ends and a pointed chin.*

PAPER PLATE PIG

Make this cheeky pig, then adapt the same method to make a whole farmyard of animals.

WHAT YOU NEED

Plain white paper plate, pink paint
Glue and glue brush
Cardboard cup, cut from an egg box
Scissors and pencil, elastic, and hole punch

1 *Cut out eye holes and a nose hole in the right place – it's a good idea to make a scrap version first to get the positions right.*

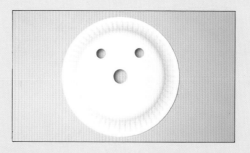

2 *Make two holes in the end of the cardboard egg cup. Then glue it onto the mask over the nose hole, and paint the whole mask pink. Stick on pink piggy ears and attach elastic to each side.*

Decorating paper

COLLECT A GOOD RANGE OF different kinds and sizes of paper. Ask people for a few sheets of writing paper, for example, and save clean wrapping paper that has come round goods or presents. There are lots of things you can do to decorate ordinary paper and make it look interesting, individual, and attractive.

PAPER AGING

Antique paper is often stiff and browny-yellow, and is great for making messages and maps look old and valuable. You can fake it with teabags!

▲ Draw a "treasure map" on the paper, using crayons in muted colours, such as brown and gray.

1 Put the teabag in the tray and pour hot water onto it. Stir the teabag round to make the water go brown. The stronger the color, the darker your paper will be.

2 Tear round the edges of the paper to make them rough. Lay the paper in the tea-water for a minute or two, until it gets stained with color.

3 Slide the paper out of the tray and hold it up for a moment to get rid of drips. Put newspaper on a flat surface, then lay the paper on it. Tape round the edges to keep the paper smooth and flat while it dries.

Torn edges stain darker, which helps the paper look authentic

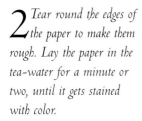

▲ Make a "proclamation" by rolling the paper up and tying it with ribbon in a bow. When you are ready to read the proclamation pull the bow.

78

MARBLING THE EASY WAY

Marbled paper is great fun to make, and can be used instead of plain paper for lots of the projects in this book. You can buy special marbling tools and paints in craft shops, but try this easy method first to get quick results.

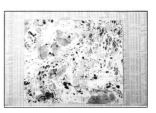

1 *Fill the tray almost to the top with water. Mix in a big splash of vinegar. Dribble up to four colors on the water. Swirl them round with a cocktail stick, or mix them by blowing gently on the surface through a straw. Drop on some extra blobs with a brush.*

2 *Gently lay the paper face-down on the surface of the water. Because the paints are thinned down, they float on top of the water. Tap over the paper very gently with your finger to get rid of any air bubbles trapped beneath it.*

3 *After a few moments, lift the paper up with both hands, holding each end and pulling it straight upwards. Hold it above the tray for a moment to let the excess water drain off.*

4 *Lay the marbled paper, colored-side up, on top of newspaper or scrap paper laid on a flat surface. Put wet masking tape round the edges of the marbled paper to keep it smooth and flat as it dries.*

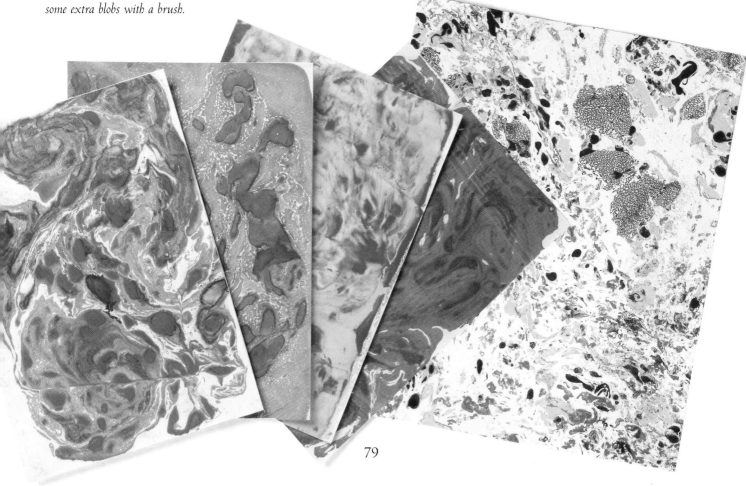

79

Special stitching

IF YOU LIKE SEWING, YOU CAN DO IT ON more than just fabric. Try decorating paper with your needle and thread. Choose stiff paper or thin card, and use embroidery threads in different colors. You could use the ideas shown here to decorate many of the objects you have made from this book.

Sew a picture onto a gift card.

Thread beads onto the stitches you make

Decorate card edges with overstitching

1 Tape some drawing paper on top of the thick paper, draw a design on the drawing paper, and sew through it to the paper beneath. Then cut off the drawing paper and throw it away.

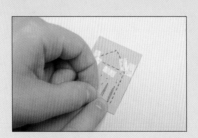

2 Alternatively, you can lightly draw a design directly onto the card, and cover it up by sewing over it. After you have finished sewing, anchor the end of the thread tightly at the back with a piece of sticky tape.

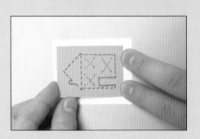

3 The back of your sewing is often a bit untidy! Finish off neatly by glueing another piece of paper or card onto the back.

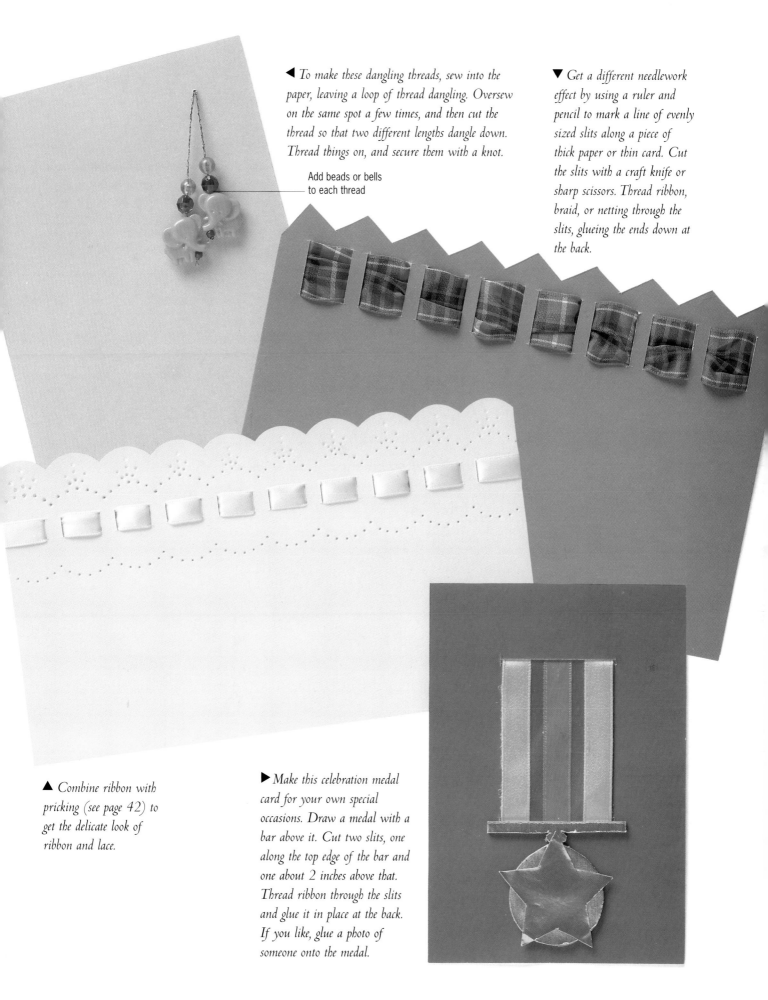

◀ To make these dangling threads, sew into the paper, leaving a loop of thread dangling. Oversew on the same spot a few times, and then cut the thread so that two different lengths dangle down. Thread things on, and secure them with a knot.

Add beads or bells
to each thread

▼ Get a different needlework effect by using a ruler and pencil to mark a line of evenly sized slits along a piece of thick paper or thin card. Cut the slits with a craft knife or sharp scissors. Thread ribbon, braid, or netting through the slits, glueing the ends down at the back.

▲ Combine ribbon with pricking (see page 42) to get the delicate look of ribbon and lace.

▶ Make this celebration medal card for your own special occasions. Draw a medal with a bar above it. Cut two slits, one along the top edge of the bar and one about 2 inches above that. Thread ribbon through the slits and glue it in place at the back. If you like, glue a photo of someone onto the medal.

Origami

ORIGAMI IS A JAPANESE WORD THAT MEANS "folding paper," an art that originated in Japan over 1,000 years ago. It can be very complicated, but the two designs shown here are simple to start with, and only need a paper square.

SWAN

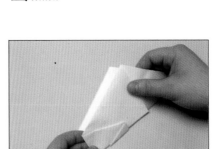

1 Lay the paper down as a diamond-shape. Make a center fold.

2 Fold the left and right corners into the center.

3 Fold the top point down to meet the inner corners in the center.

4 Fold the point up 1.5 inches to make a tab.

5 Fold the model in half with the "wings" on the outside.

6 Pull up the head and neck so the swan stands up.

Draw a face on your swan.

82

PAPER PLAY BALL

Hang the ball by a loop to make a decoration

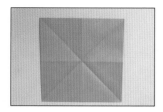

1 *Start with a square of thin paper. Make valley folds down and across. Make diagonal mountain folds between the corners.*

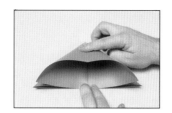

2 *Pull up the middle and push either side in to make a triangle.*

3 *Working with the front layer of paper, fold the two bottom corners up to the top center.*

4 *Turn the model over, and fold the other two corners up.*

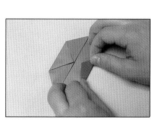

5 *Working with one layer, fold the left and right corners into the middle.*

6 *Turn the model over and repeat step 5.*

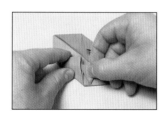

7 *Working with one layer, fold down the two top corners and tuck them in to the tops of the triangles beneath. Turn the model over and repeat.*

8 *Blow into the hole at the bottom end to make the ball inflate.*

▲ *Play with the ball, or blow it along with a straw.*

▲ *Run the bottom hole of the bomb under the tap to fill it with water — then throw it quickly!*

83

Origami butterfly

TRADITIONAL ORIGAMI BECAME A real art in Japan, with incredibly beautiful and complicated objects being made. What most origami objects have in common is that you can usually do something with them – either play with them, or make them move.

BUTTERFLY

This butterfly may look difficult, but it just takes care and patience. You might like to practice first on some scrap paper until you get the folds absolutely right. Then choose some thin but strong paper for the final model.

1 *Fold the square in half lengthwise and widthwise. Unfold it, and turn it over so that you can see two mountain folds.*

2 *Fold the paper diagonally both ways, so that you have two valley folds.*

3 *Pull the two points shown upward and inward to make a triangle shape.*

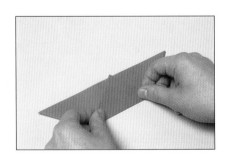

4 *Fold the bottom point up to meet the top edge.*

5 *Fold the two bottom corners in a little, as shown in the picture.*

6 *Unfold these corners again, making sure that the creases hold in the paper.*

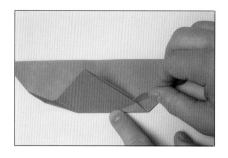

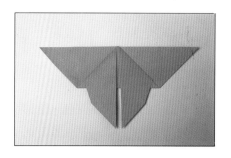

7 Partly unfold the top, so that you can fold the inner layers only of the bottom corners in again. The previous creases should make this easy.

8 Pull down the top layer by holding the left and right corners and pulling them down to the center.

9 This is the shape you should now have. You can see the butterfly shape beginning to appear.

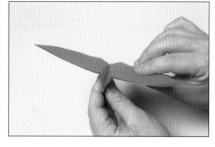

10 Pinch up the middle of the butterfly's "body."

11 Fold the body out in a V-shape, on either side of the center.

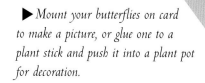

▶ Mount your butterflies on card to make a picture, or glue one to a plant stick and push it into a plant pot for decoration.

Craft festivities

Many of the crafts covered in this book can be adapted to a particular theme, such as yearly festivals in your religion. Here are some ideas for Christmas. You'll probably think of all sorts of other adaptations to the crafts shown in the book, to suit particular occasions.

WHAT YOU NEED
....

Medium-weight shiny, colored paper

Scissors

Cotton thread

Glue

Hang up bows and bells by loops of thread

BOWS AND BELLS

Pleated bows and bells made out of pretty paper can be used to decorate presents or hung up for display.

1 To make a bell, cut a circle of paper, then mark a line into the middle from the edge, and cut along it.

2 Pleat around the middle, and then glue the edges together with thread running down through the middle. Knot the thread inside the bell to keep it in place.

1 For a bow, cut a rectangle of paper. A wide rectangle will make a "bunchy" bow; a longer rectangle will give you a longer bow.

2 Make narrow pleats along the long edge. Pinch the pleats together and tie thread tightly round the middle. Then fan out the pleats on either side.

▶ *If your festival is Christmas, add shiny gold and silver bells to your Christmas tree.*

▶ *Many of the projects for party decorations can also be used for festivities, like this banner chain.*

◀ *Why not make special gift tags for your presents? You could make them match your other decorations or the wrapping paper you have made.*

▶ *Use the method shown on page 19 to make a festive gift frame for a photograph, a picture, or a piece of your own art.*

87

Papermaking

Y OU CAN RECYCLE OLD SCRAP PAPER AND card to make your very own new paper. It's great fun to try, and you can add flat objects such as pictures or leaves to the recycled paper to make it more unusual.

WHICH PAPER?

The paper scraps you use will determine the color and texture of the finished new paper sheet. Use writing paper or typing paper, tissue, and card. Don't use newspaper (it goes brown), or paper with a shiny coating on.

MOLD AND DECKLE

To make paper you need a mold and a deckle. The mold is a wooden frame with netting stretched over it. The deckle is a second wooden frame without the netting. The mold catches the pulp and the deckle holds it in place. You can buy a mold from a craft shop, but it isn't difficult to make your own.

1 Cut a piece of netting about 2 inches bigger than the picture frame all round.

2 Stretch the netting over the frame, and secure it all round the edges with drawing pins, pulling it tight and even. Here you can see the covered mold and the uncovered deckle.

Making paper can be pretty messy, so make sure that all your work surfaces are well protected, and that you wear an apron. Try in small quantities first, until you get good at it.

1 Soak the paper pieces in water for about an hour to soften them. Strain off the excess water. Fill the blender three-quarters full of water and add 10–15 wet paper pieces per pint. Switch on and blend until the pulp is smooth and creamy — about 30 seconds. Make six loads and pour them into the plastic bowl.

2 Stir the pulp so that all the fibers don't sink to the bottom. Hold the mold firmly with the deckle aligned on top of it (if you are using one), and the netting in between. Stand them up at the back of the bowl with the deckle toward you.

3 Gently slide the mold and deckle down into the bowl toward you, until they are lying flat under the liquid pulp.

WRITE ON!

If you want to be able to write on your paper, you need to add "size" to the soggy paper pulp in the bowl before you mold it. This will stop ink from soaking into the paper surface when you write on the finished paper. Add two teaspoons of cold water starch to the bowl, and stir it in to the pulp.

4 After a few moments, pull the mold and deckle straight up out of the water. The pulp will lie evenly on top of the netting. Shake it gently from side to side, and then back and forth, to spread the paper fibers.

5 Carefully lift the deckle away, taking care not to drag it over the pulp. Turn to the next page to see how you get the paper out of the mold and dry it.

Finishing paper

THE BEST WAY OF GETTING THE WET PAPER PULP out of the frame is by a process called couching (pronounced "kootching.") Although it can be the most tricky part of papermaking, it is essential if the sheet is to end up flat. The trick to successful couching and drying is simply not to rush!

COUCHING

Couching is the trick of squeezing enough water out of the wet paper pulp to allow it to fall easily out of the mold. Be patient, though – you will find that the wet paper sticks to the mold and will tear easily if not handled carefully.

1 Lay out two dry absorbent cloths on the covered work surface. Lay the mold on top and cover with two more cloths. Pat the sandwich gently until the blotters are wet. Replace with dry blotters.

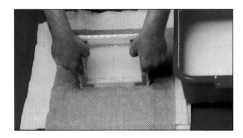

2 Continue doing this until the paper begins to come away from the mold when a corner is gently pulled. When it is ready, lay the mold on a new dry cloth, press down firmly and then ease the mold away, leaving the pulp behind.

DRYING

Don't be tempted to hurry this process up by applying heat, because that would make the paper very bumpy and uneven.

1 Lay more dry cloths on top of the new paper, then place it between the middle pages of a newspaper. Put a board on top and weight it down with something heavy. Leave to dry. After a few hours, remove the outer layer of cloths from the newspaper and replace with fresh dry cloths and more newspaper.

2 Weight them with books as before, and leave to dry again. Repeat this process every six hours or so until the paper is completely dry. Then open the cloths and slip a palette knife (or an ordinary knife) under the edge of the paper all round.

ADDING THE FINISHING TOUCH

Once you have begun papermaking you will be able to experiment in lots of different ways. You could add texture to a sheet by drying it under a knobbly cloth. You might like to make extra-thick fibrous paper, or fine, thin sheets. And you can press fine, textured things like leaves into the paper while it dries.

▶ *Some hand-made papers are so beautiful, they become works of art all on their own, so frame them!*

3 *Holding one edge, peel off the cloth. Be careful not to bend the paper, which might damage it.*

4 *The paper is now finished! You can put more than one sheet of pulp under the same board, as long as you put plenty of kitchen cloths and newspaper in between each sheet.*

▶ *Mount hand-made paper on card to make your own stationery.*

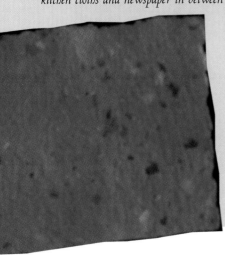

◀ *Finished pieces of homemade paper have a wonderful texture. The uneven edges just add to the effect.*

Index

Page numbers in *italic* refer to illustrations or captions on those pages.

A

aging paper 78, *78*
airplanes 20-1, *20-1*
animals, papier mache 56, *56-7*

B

bags 51, *51*
balloon masks, papier mache 54, *54*
balls, origami *83*
baskets, woven 40, *40-1*
bells *86*
boas *71*
boats 22-23, *22-23*
bow ties 72, *72*
bowls, papier mache 55, *55*
bows:
    paper chains *49*
    pleated paper 86, *86*
boxes:
    gift basket box 50, *50*
    storage boxes 52, *52-3*
butterfly, origami 84, *84-5*

C

card *11*
cards:
    castle card 31, *31*
    dinner dress card 48, *48*
    pop-up cards 28, *28-29*
    poster cards 32, *32-3*
    secret doors 30, *30*
    teddy-in-the-box setting cards 48, *48*
    whirling wheel 31, *31*
carp kite 65, *65*
castle card 31, *31*
caveman outfit 71, *71*
chancer 45, *45*
Chinese hats 67, *67*
Christmas 86, *86-87*
clothes 70-3, *70-3*
collage 34-7, *34-7*
concertina card 16, *16*
cone hats 66, *66*
cone person 24, *24*
corrugated cardboard *11*
couching, papermaking 90, *90*
crepe paper *10*
curling 13, *13*
curves, weaving 39, *39*
cut-out chain 49, *49*
cutting 13, *13*
cutting mats *11*
cylinder person 24, *24*

D

darts 20, *20*
deckle, papermaking 88, *88*
decorating paper 78-9, *78-9*
decorations, party 46-7, *46-7*
dinner dress card 48, *48*
dresses 70-1, *70-1*
drying paper 90, *90-1*

E

envelopes:
    decorating 59, *59*
    weaving *38*
eye mask 74, *74*

F

fancy dress clothes 70-1, *70-1*
fans 17, *17*
festivals 86, *86-7*
fibers *10*
firebird mask 75, *75*
flowers:
    folded 15, *15*
    tissue 62-3, *62-3*
folding 12, *12*
    flowers 15, *15*
    origami 82-5, *82-5*
frames *87*
    collage 36, *36-7*
    pricking 43, *43*
    quilling 19, *19*
full face masks 76, *76-7*

G

games 45, *45*
gift bags 51, *51*
gift basket box 50, *50*
gift tags *18*
gluing, pop-up cards *29*
grain *10*

H

handmade paper *11*, 88-91, *88-91*
hanging heart 39, *39*
hats 66-9, *66-9*
headband hats 68, *68*
heart, hanging 39, *39*
helicopter, spinning 21, *21*

J

Japanese paper *10*

K

kite, carp 65, *65*

L

lace-up wallet 58, *58*
letter lady 26, *26*

M

making paper 88-91, *88-91*
marbling 79, *79*
masks 74-7, *74-7*
mini-baskets 40, *40-1*
mini-people 27, *27*
mirror, collage frame 36, *36-7*
models, papier mache 56, *56-7*
molds:
    papermaking 88, *88*
    papier mache 54-5, *54-5*
mosaic 37, *37*
mountain folds *12*, 14

N

napkin rings 47, *47*
napkins:
    decorating 47, *47*
    folding 46, *46*

O

origami 82-5, *82-5*

P

paper chains 49, *49*
paper plate pig 77, *77*
papermaking 88-91, *88-91*
papier mache 54-7, *54-7*
party decorations 46-9, *46-9*
party sticks 63, *63*
people 24-7, *24-7*
photo frame 19, *19*
picture tab paper 61, *61*
pictures:
    pricking 42, *42-3*
    quilling 18, *18*
pig, paper plate 77, *77*
planes 20-1, *20-1*
pleating 12, *12*
bows and bells 86, *86*
concertina card 16, *16*
cutting 14, *14*

fans 17, *17*
folded flowers 15, *15*
pop-up cards 28-9, *28-9*
poster cards 32, *32-3*
pricking 42-3, *42-3*
printing stationery 60, *60*
puppets, shadow 64, *64*

Q

quilling 18-19, *18-19*

R

recycled paper *11*
rigged sailing ship 23, *23*
rimmed hats 68, *68*
roses, tissue 63, *63*

S

sailing ships 23, *23*, 42, *42-3*
scoring 12, *12*
secret doors card 30, *30*
setting cards, teddy-in-the-box 48,
    48
shadow puppets 64, *64*
shirts, false 73, *73*
size, papermaking 89
spinning helicopter 21, *21*
stationery 58-61, *58-61*
stencil card *11*
stencils, napkin decorations 47, *47*
stitching 80, *80-1*
storage boxes 52, *52-3*
stretching paper 34, *34*
stunt plane 21, *21*
sun caps 69, *69*
swan, origami 82, *82*

T

table decorations 46-7, *46-7*
teddy bear, papier mache 57, *57*
teddy-in-the-box setting cards 48,
    48

texture, papermaking 91, *91*
theaters 25, *25*
tissue paper *10*
    collage 35, *35*
    flowers 62-3, *62-3*
    party sticks 63, *63*
    roses 63, *63*
tools 11, *11*
topiary flower tree 62, *62*
toys 44, *44*
tracing paper *11*
tube dress 70, *70*
twenties dress 71, *71*

V

valley folds *12*, 14
Venetian firebird mask 75, *75*

W

waistcoats 72, *72*
wallet, lace-up 58, *58*
weaving 38-41, *38-41*
whirling wheel card 31, *31*
windmill, whirly 44, *44*

Z

zigzags, weaving 39, *39*